Voices from the Margins

Consensus building and planning with the poor in Bangladesh

Roger Lewins, Stuart Coupe
and Francis Murray

PRACTICAL ACTION
Publishing

Intermediate Technology Publications Ltd
trading as Practical Action Publishing
Schumacher Centre for Technology and Development
Bourton on Dunsmore, Rugby,
Warwickshire CV23 9QZ, UK
www.practicalactionpublishing.org

© Intermediate Technology Publications Ltd, 2007

First published in 2007

ISBN 978 1 85339 624 3

307.
14095
LEW

A catalogue record for this book is available from the British Library.

Since 1974, Practical Action Publishing has published and disseminated
books and information in support of international development work
throughout the world. Practical Action Publishing (formerly ITDG
Publishing) is a trading name of Intermediate Technology Publications Ltd
(Company Reg. No. 1159018), the wholly owned publishing company of
Intermediate Technology Development Group Ltd (working name Practical
Action). Practical Action Publishing trades only in support of its parent
charity objectives and any profits are covenanted back to Practical Action
(Charity Reg. No. 247257, Group VAT Registration No. 880 9924 76).

Cover design by Mercer Design
Indexed by Indexing Specialists
Typeset by SJI Services
Printed by Replika Press

Contents

Foreword

'Participation' has sometimes been seen as a panacea or a 'technical fix' for natural resource management. But all too often large-scale participatory approaches have failed because of inequitable rights of access, use and control over natural resources, macro-economic policy or corporate interests. Many practitioners have thus increasingly learnt to see 'participation' as part of, and dependent on, wider structural changes towards more equitable people-centred processes and democracy. In this vision of the future, 'participation' and 'transformation' are mutually reinforcing dynamics. And with a growing focus on governance and democracy, the place of methods in participatory learning and action is being gradually reassessed. Indeed, there is some evidence for a shift from the earlier technical focus (methods, skills and tools) to a more political focus (agenda setting, changing institutions and organizations). Whilst still important, methodological issues are now increasingly seen in the context of a more relational understanding of participation in which power and knowledge are centre stage.

This gradual shift to a more critically reflexive approach that links participation with power, knowledge and citizenship is good news for people and the environment. But a relational understanding of participation does not diminish the importance of participatory methods for learning and action. Critical assessments of methodological innovations continue to be needed to improve the theory and practice of participation and people-centred processes in natural resource management. This book focuses on one such innovation – Participatory Action Plan Development (PAPD) for natural resource management in Bangladesh.

From a sustainable livelihoods perspective, there are two main challenges in managing natural resources and ecosystems. One is to respond appropriately to the ecological dynamics of a given environment, preserving its resilience and functions while assuring a flow of benefits from it. This challenge is mostly about *content* – the *what* and *when* of managing natural resources and ecosystems at different scales. The other is to respond to the social characteristics of the same environment, dealing in an effective way with the inevitably conflicting interests and concerns of different social actors. This challenge is mostly about *process* – the *who* and *how* of managing natural resources and environments. Throughout history, attempts to respond to the latter social challenge have included many forms of hostile struggle, both open and violent and hidden, via various means of social control. Fortunately, they also include a variety of collaborative, co-management solutions based on negotiated agreements on the roles, rights, responsibilities and benefits of different social actors.

By focussing on the strengths and weaknesses of PAPD the authors enrich our understanding of this tradition of collaborative management among multiple actors. They offer a critical and useful analysis of the PAPD as used with, and by, marginalized communities in the Bangladesh charlands.

The authors have written a book for practitioners. They describe in clear language the specific features of this dynamic process of participatory planning and negotiation for consensus building in natural resource management. It is refreshing to read an account that seeks to promote a flexible process rather than a step-by-step methodology toolkit approach to consensus building. The approach described in this book relies on light but skilful facilitation, with no fixed timetable for reaching consensus. As the authors argue, PAPD needs to work alongside what NGOs and government agencies are already doing, whilst promoting the use of informal institutions and key social actors to work things out. The approach encourages community groups to make their own connections and form new relationships with enabling institutions and service providers in pursuit of village plans. Planning here is a means to develop social and political linkages for change.

Among the valuable lessons and reminders offered in this book, the following are particularly noteworthy:

- First, eliciting and making visible diverse local realities, priorities, categories and indicators through participatory learning and planning is still very much needed today to challenge top-down, 'one size fits all' science, policy and practice in natural resource management. Acknowledging and building on diversity within the social and ecological realm is a key challenge for equity and sustainability throughout the world.
- Second, collective action, based on social learning and negotiated agreements among relevant actors in an ecosystem, is a condition for sustainable local livelihoods. Platforms that bring relevant actors together are key in mobilizing capacity for social learning, negotiation and collective action for natural resource management and for building livelihood assets and access to them by the poor.
- Third, indicators of 'success' need to emphasize informal institutional change – continued interaction with other social actors and secondary stakeholders and new relationships (processes) – as much as the longevity of visible structures (project-related committees, for instance) or the frequency of formal meetings. Facilitators must therefore seek a wider and deeper understanding of the informal institutional setting.
- And last but not least, local and existing institutions continue to be neglected in mainstream environment and development policy and practice. For sure, local formal and informal institutions are not always equitable and inclusive. Yet they can provide an important basis for more diverse forms of endogenous development that depart from current hegemonic thinking and practice. Building on local organizations and institutions is key for negotiated transformations and making 'better worlds' possible for everyone.

Facilitating and encouraging individual and collective learning for inclusive and equitable participation requires action at various levels, including not only the local but also the national and international contexts. This is where the real constraints on the spread, scaling up and mainstreaming of the participatory process very often lie. The authors and their organization – Practical Action – have chosen to focus on a microcosm, drawing lessons from participatory planning and consensus building in Bangladesh. As such, they are encouraging valuable learning within their own organization and beyond, inviting us to critically reflect and learn with them.

Dr Michel Pimbert
Director
Sustainable Agriculture, Biodiversity and Livelihoods Programme
International Institute for Environment and Development (IIED), UK

List of tables

List of figures

List of boxes

List of photographs

Acronyms and glossary

ACR	alternative conflict resolution
ADC	Additional District Commissioner
ADR	alternative dispute resolution
AKIS	Agricultural Knowledge and Information Systems
beel	shallow lake
bongsho	a large community assemblage consisting of separate *gusthi*
CAP	community action plan
CBO	community-based organization
chars	riverine sandbars prone to periodic erosion and accretion
CNRS	Centre for Natural Resource Studies
CPR	common property resource
DFID	Department for International Development (UK)
DIPs	deliberative inclusionary processes
FCPPA	Framework for Consensus Participation in Protected Areas
GO	government organization
Gram Sharkar	'village government' – lowest tier of formal government
gusthi	a patrilineal kinship group or clan
IUCN	The International Union for the Conservation of Nature
jalmohal	a state-registered waterbody
jama't	a religious congregation at a small mosque local mosque
jama't masjid	Friday mosque – larger mosque hosting main weekly service
jotedars	middlemen/rich peasants
kabiraj	traditional healer
khas/khasland	government owned common lands
masjid	a mosque
masjid committee	a committee for mosque-related or secular functions
mathbor	respected community member acting as arbitrator in *salish*
MCA	multi-criteria analysis
MCBC	Managing Conflict and Building Consensus (in rural livelihoods projects)

NGO	non-governmental organization
NRM	natural resource management
NRSP	Natural Resource Systems Programme of DFID
PAPD	Participatory Action Plan Development
para	a village neighbourhood; often a cluster of homesteads
PIPs	policies, institutions and processes
PRA	participatory rural appraisal
PTD	participatory technology development
RAAKS	Rapid Appraisal of Agricultural Knowledge Systems
RCE	rural community extensionist
RDSM	Rural Development and Social Mobilization – partner NGO
RMI	resource management institution
salish	traditional local conflict resolution mechanism
samaj	a residential brotherhood – often based around the mosque
STEPS	A planning tool to uncover key social, technical, economic, political and sustainability precursors to local action
Taka/Tk.	Unit of currency in Bangladesh
UACC	Upazila Agricultural Coordination Committee
UP	Union Parishad – lowest administrative boundary in Bangladesh, usually 4–5 villages
Upazila	second administrative tier consisting of multiple unions
WBMC	waterbody management committee

Acknowledgements

We would like to acknowledge the considerable efforts of all those who have been involved in developing, testing and applying the PAPD approach in Bangladesh and elsewhere. We are particularly grateful to the originators of PAPD – Julian Barr, Mokhlesur Rahman, Anisul Islam and Peter Dixon – for their encouragement to produce this book and to Muhamed Ali of Practical Action Bangladesh and his team for their enlightening work with char communities. Thanks to Julian and Peter for comments on early versions of the text on consensus theory and to Barnaby Peacocke and colleagues at Practical Action UK for their advice and suggestions during the research and writing.

This publication is funded by the Natural Resources Systems Programme of the UK Department for International Development as an output of 'Consensus for a holistic approach to improve rural livelihoods in riverine islands of Bangladesh' (Project R8103).

Introduction

The demand from both donors and governments to increase the impact of rural development initiatives is as strong as ever. Developing country governments are under pressure to halt environmental degradation, increase food security and meet poverty elimination targets while donors and other implementing agencies must now justify existing policies and approaches in terms of value and coverage. Given several decades of project-based interventions, however, there are still few examples of widely dispersed successes. Unfortunately, where development activities have resulted in long-term beneficial change they have tended to occur as isolated events, with limited geographic spread and influence.

One of the principal reasons for these disappointing results has been the over-reliance on a 'blueprint' approach to implementation that has failed to allow space for the poor to shape interventions and make them relevant to their specific needs. This has given rise to a counter-movement within the development sector, promoting much greater involvement of local stakeholders in agenda setting and planning. In turn, this has influenced governments and service delivery organizations to embrace a participatory approach within policy and practice.

Despite efforts to engage the poor in the development process, however, new initiatives tend to be externally driven and a 'participatory approach' is often grafted onto pre-existing objectives and modus operandi. This may be true of both the performance of government stakeholders and service providers and local level stakeholders where community-based management may be played out within pre-established power networks and 'rules of the game'.

In the case of natural resource management (NRM) in the floodplain of Bangladesh, agencies associated with specific sectors have utilized a range of models to accommodate local participation, whilst pursuing agency or project objectives. In general, agencies tend to adopt a mechanistic approach to participation with predetermined structures, responsibilities and roles. What is often overlooked by technical experts, however, is that rural communities will often have their own mechanisms to accommodate different perspectives and to reach decisions to enact 'local initiatives' in NRM (see Table 1.1).

A participation process, worthy of the name, rarely reaches the most vulnerable and marginalized, people whose social and political status suppresses their voice and excludes them from new opportunities. There is a desperate need to move from the participation rhetoric of projects and policy towards practice that really allows unexpected, complicated and sometimes inconvenient outcomes. In most cases the disparity between donor and government pronouncements

Table 0.1   Stereotypical participatory approaches within the natural resource sectors in Bangladesh

	Fisheries sector	Water sector	Environment sector	*Local initiatives*
Facilitator	GO and/or NGO	GO and/or NGO	GO and/or NGO	Respected elders (*mathbor*) and landowners
Participation type*	Group formation and light support	Group formation and planning	Continuous, advisory	Self-mobilization
Purpose	Increased fish production	Flood management and increased agriculture	Habitat management, biodiversity	Seasonal fisheries vs farm trade-offs
Structures	Fixed groups	Fixed, hierarchical groups	Resource management & new income generating groups	Ad hoc meetings sometimes within mosque committee

*These 'types' acknowledge Pimbert and Pretty's (1994) classification of participation that focuses on the role of the actual participant. These roles range from *passive participation,* where stakeholders are totally directed, to *self-mobilization or active participation* where people undertake initiatives in isolation from a third party. (Modified from Lewins, 2004.)

on the issue and the reality on the ground is marked, or as in the Bangladeshi proverb;

> *Kazir guru ketaba acheye, kintu goaleye nei!*
> *(Kazi's cow is in the book, but not in the shed!)*

An important step in addressing weaknesses in the participation process is recognizing the diversity of local interests and agenda that operate at the local level. There are encouraging signs that the notion of the 'community' as a fixed and harmonious entity is being abandoned by donors, policy formers and other facilitators of development. What appears to be missing is an attempt to better understand pre-existing institutions and to make room for approaches that build consensus, rather than inadvertently introduce conflict.

Local planning that can accommodate this diversity and that looks to include those outside the normal suite of target beneficiaries is most likely to be perceived as legitimate and to have lasting impacts. New consensus can then help overcome social and institutional obstacles to pro-poor change associated with natural resource management and rural development, more generally.

This book introduces a participatory approach suited to catalysing change for the poor in challenging social and political environments. It draws from research in Bangladesh intended to develop and apply a consensus-building methodology that can release the democratic energies of communities living in highly vulnerable conditions.

PAPD has evolved from several research- and community-based natural resource management projects in Bangladesh. PAPD draws on a range of useful tools commonly used within participatory rural appraisal but takes as its starting point the need to understand conflict and consensus and to develop social capital and institutional linkage. The uptake of PAPD in Bangladesh has been encouraging, the methodology spreading from the floodplain and fisheries context where it was first developed into the coastal setting, forests and broader rural development and flood-preparedness initiatives.

In 2002 Practical Action attempted using PAPD with the very vulnerable communities in the isolated charlands of Bangladesh. The experience led to a modified approach, intended to release the planning potential of communities, but to allow informal and formal institutions to gravitate towards the process and to work with the poor within a realistic timeframe.

Crucially, the intention of this book is not to promote a formulaic methodology but to present a working approach that encourages innovation and modification by facilitators and participants. Acknowledging the key stages in consensus building should provide a basis for working and reviewing progress but without limiting prospects for adaptation or reducing relevance to the poor.

Chapter 1 reviews the origins and development of consensus-building methodologies in natural resource management through to their refinement for use in marginal and vulnerable areas in Bangladesh. Chapter 2 outlines experience with PAPD in the chars of Jamalpur, Bangladesh, where Practical Action has worked with marginalized communities for several years. Crucially, the facilitators of the process took time to understand the role of informal institutions and local family groups (*gusthi*) in blocking or supporting alternative community plans. Chapter 3 demonstrates the special features of char-modified PAPD, an approach that retains the key consensus building stages and strategies but which unfolds at a pace intended to build trust and sustainable linkages between the poor and external stakeholders. The book concludes with a discussion of the potential for participatory and consensual planning like PAPD and where such approaches might be realistically positioned and supported.

1

Conflict resolution and consensus building for natural resource management and development

The role of conflict resolution and consensus building in development has undergone several key changes over the last two decades but remains strongly associated with natural resource management (NRM). As donors, governments and other development partners become more aware of the complexity of NRM and its relationship to poverty, both the purpose and approach of interventions has evolved to reflect changing development objectives and new knowledge.

Recent approaches to consensus building for NRM have attempted to bypass the limitations of project-driven development and have attempted the joint identification of development opportunities that might outlive external facilitation. Rather than a tool to smooth the implementation of pre-determined project activities, there is a growing recognition that participatory consensus building that actively engages multiple interests might help produce lasting change by forging new social and institutional relationships.

As the focus of this book, Participatory Action Plan Development (PAPD) draws on recent advancements in thinking about rural livelihoods and interpreting local development – in particular, issues relating to the heterogeneity and meaning of 'community' and notions of social and political capital.

The principles of consensus

It is useful to introduce the notion of consensus with a simple theoretical definition of conflict. In the context of NRM, conflict can be simply regarded as a situation where a strong and persistent divergence of positions (needs, values etc.) among users and other stakeholders presents an obstacle to managing a specific area or natural resource (Rijsberman, 1999). Conflicting parties will tend to defend their own interests but the duration, intensity and end points of conflict are a reflection of other more subtle motivations of the individual or group. Simple theories of conflict have assumed material self interest and individualistic behaviour but Pruitt and Rubin's (1986) 'dual concern' model incorporates the interest each party has for the welfare of the other, incorporating an ethical or civic perspective to the behaviour of social actors in communities. The model is useful because it acknowledges that conflict is neither static nor permanent and can result in one of several outcomes (Figure 1.1).

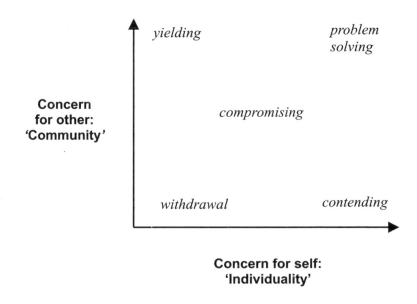

Figure 1.1   The dual concern model with the five basic responses to conflict (after Pruitt and Rubin, 1986).

Of these five end points, the position or outcome of 'problem solving' is the most desirable because it is the most likely to result in long-term solutions to conflict. 'Problem solving' can be viewed as a positive-sum game because the total size of the benefits to be gained is not fixed, but can grow according to the quality of the process of negotiation or discussion. By contrast, 'compromise' is better represented as a zero-sum game where the outcome of negotiation is to shift benefits (sovereignty of territory, the right to practice traditional livelihoods etc.) from one party to another (Pruitt and Carnevale, 1993).

The product of successful problem solving, then, is *consensus* i.e. agreement whereby *all* stakeholders perceive their position to be strengthened (Warner, 1999).

If this outcome does not evolve endogenously, third party *conflict resolution* may be required to address the fundamental interests of all groups and remove the source of conflict permanently (Miall et al., 1999). Alternatively, *conflict management* could be deployed to limit or direct the course of conflict by actively enhancing actors' capacity to deal with economic, environmental, social or political change. Rijsberman (1999) describes a continuum of conflict management approaches that reflect the nature of third party intervention (Figure 1.2). The approaches range from *consensus building*, where the role of a third party as mediator may be negligible and outcomes or agreements may be flexible and informal, to *binding assistance*, a top-down process where a third party acts as arbitrator rather than mediator. Outcomes in this case are often termed 'agreements' and tend to be legal or contractual in nature (see Figure 1.2).

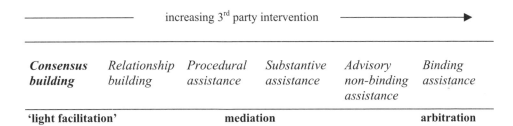

Figure 1.2   A continuum of conflict management approaches. (after Rijsberman (1999), Moore and Priscoli (1989), Priscoli (1990) and MacNaughton and Brune (1997).)

It could be argued that some of the more mechanistic decision-making tools that have been applied to NRM problems help to achieve compromise rather than consensus. Multi-criteria analysis (MCA), for instance, attempts to mathematically reconcile the diversity of stakeholder opinions and objectives. The various management objectives (i.e. ecological, social, economic) are weighted and best-fit management strategies are calculated. However, the trade-offs calculated by MCA rely on 'satisficing' (essentially identifying strategies by upsetting the least number – or least important – of stakeholders). As such they represent 'finding compromise' rather than 'reaching consensus' through problem solving. The application of MCA in the development context is also limited by its reliance on neatly bounded management and policy options and large and reliable sets of data.

Recently trade-off analysis has incorporated a participatory approach to planning meetings and local consultation. However, processes such as these are dependent on respondents having access to sufficient information and having a good and accurate understanding of the potential impact of alternative management scenarios on their livelihoods. In addition, the development of best-fit management plans through balancing stakeholder objectives may not increase the level of understanding between stakeholders and their underlying interests (an indicator of 'good' consensus building – see Box 1.1).

Consensus building then, can be considered as just one of several tools for the management of conflict (Warner, 1999), but as conflict management at its most participatory and locale specific. In contrast to the force, avoidance and compromise that characterizes conflict resolution or binding approaches, consensus building attempts agreement through co-learning and 'mutual gains'. In other words, consensus building creates a situation whereby all participants benefit from the process. As such it is based on a concept of community as a 'heterogeneous whole' in which there are stakeholders with varied needs, livelihoods interests, goals and perspectives of NRM.

Finally, consensus can be built in the absence of pre-existing conflict. Rather than a means to overcome disputes, sensitive and well-informed facilitation can function to garner mutual support for collective plans and activities where local potential is constrained by access to social and political influence.

Framing the principles of conflict and consensus this way provides the basis to discuss and evaluate the various approaches that have evolved in the context of NRM and elsewhere.

The origins of conflict resolution and consensus building methods

The principles of conflict resolution and consensus building that have been applied in the development context have their origins in the developed world and in particular the USA. Interestingly, these principles were first applied to local and corporate decision making and were later subsumed within government-facilitated processes.

The early experiences with deliberate and democratic forms of consensus building stemmed directly from the American civil rights and environment movements of the 1960s and 1970s that promoted racial and sexual equality and environmental awareness. Community groups in the USA were challenging the traditional conventions of oppositional debate associated with party politics and in doing so replaced it with a new emphasis on informality and flexibility. In effect, the goal shifted from one of reaching a single decision in time (a motion in favour of one party at the expense of another) to that of collective agreement and improved relations between the participants.

Originally an attempt to bypass government, some of these key principles went on to be applied in other contexts and even to be embraced by the state. In the late 1970s, for instance, regional programmes in the USA were promoting mediation within schools or in 'neighbourhood justice centres'. In the 1980s, business adopted similar principles to avoid costly litigation and the normal legal processes by internalizing their dispute resolution. Consensus building in this context has been termed alternative dispute resolution (ADR), reflecting the demand for negotiation processes outside the formal structures of government and courts of law.

In the 1990s, the role of non-expert (or non-elite) public groups in both the developed and the developing world expanded from one of single-issue dispute resolution to a more general contribution to the decision-making process. This new role was partly in response to growing public cynicism and what was seen as increasing alienation from the democratic process and the apparent inability of the market or the state to resolve complex environmental issues. In parallel, space was being made for new modes of environmental governance, nationally and internationally (e.g. the emphasis on local stakeholder or citizen groups in Local Agenda 21 after Rio 1992).

Holmes and Scoones (2000) have undertaken an extensive review of the role and character of these deliberative inclusionary processes (DIPs). A wide range of DIPs exist, including neighbourhood fora, citizen's juries, consensus conferences, deliberative polling, multi-criteria mapping and public meetings. These processes may function with or without the support of the state but the political space for them to operate is often created by government. DIPs, in the context of environmental decision-making, often takes place at the level of local government and with central support. The state, in turn, gains greater perceived legitimacy in policy and planning and the benefits derived through increased public support and compliance (Pelletier et al., 1999).

Characteristics of the approaches and recent developments

Although ADR processes vary according to their setting (civic, environmental, corporate etc.) they all share a common emphasis on informality and direct and equal participation by all stakeholder groups. In consequence, compliance and satisfaction with ADR negotiated settlements tends to exceed those reached through formal legal means. ADR achieves this by reducing the emphasis on written rules and evidence to a minimum and by encouraging openness, information sharing and face-to-face relations between the parties.[1]

By introducing consensus building to a new audience and set of users, ADR has encouraged a proliferation of approaches and progressive thinking on dispute resolution. A recurrent theme in ADR (and a mantra for facilitators and mediators) has been the emphasis on understanding disputes from the perspectives of the contesting parties. In order to gain a constructive outcome such as consensus, any third party must understand what motivates the groups in the dispute. Crucially, the need to separate positions from interests is stressed repeatedly in the ADR literature. In their influential work *Getting to Yes*, Fisher and Ury (1981) state:

Interests motivate people; they are the silent movers behind the hubbub of positions. Your position is something you have decided upon. Your interests are what caused you to so decide. Reconciling interests rather than positions works for two reasons. First, for every interest there usually exist several possible positions that could satisfy it. All too often people simply adopt the most obvious position…

Several of the consensus building principles used within ADR have been applied specifically to resolve management problems in focussed planning fora. The approach known as Future Search does this to help communities and organizations find common ground for action. Future Search was developed in the USA but has also been applied in the UK to help implement county-level planning within Local Agenda 21 (Walker, 1999).[2] The methodology attempts to involve relatively large numbers of people to improve discrete systems and overcome management problems by bringing together a representative range of stakeholders large enough to assemble a 'whole system' under one roof.

Although Future Search is a particularly structured manifestation of ADR principles, with several planning stages each allocated a set period of time, the underlying objective is to give a broad cross section of a community greater control over the process of local change. Future Search attempts this by first reviewing the past and acknowledging the views of the participants (Weisbord and Janoff, 1995). Considering present issues then helps explore the key local trends and issues that impact the various stakeholders before people are asked to 'vote' for the trends that they consider the most pressing. The key characteristic of Future Search, though, is the way it attempts to bypass entrenched positions or 'business as usual' by encouraging participants to envision idealized future scenarios and the pathways or plans with which to achieve them. Conflicts between stakeholders are acknowledged, but 'put on hold' so that participants can focus on common ground. The final stage of these conferences generates short- and long-term action plans to help realize these envisioned futures for all stakeholders. Groups canvas support for their suggestions and report back to an open plenary intended to provide opportunities for groups to collaborate across traditional boundaries. The final step of the Future Search conference seeks the commitment of participants in undertaking specific actions and encourages them to take responsibility for their own projects. The agreed plans are recorded to help maintain action and public commitment to change.

As a consensus-building methodology, Future Search has the benefit of being inclusive, transparent and treating all participants as peers. It purposely avoids trying to resolve present conflicts by asking participants to focus on the future, to switch their attention from present difficulties and to focus on the common ground between them. In this respect, it is an empowering methodology, requiring careful facilitation but equipping participants with the confidence and plans to take responsibility for their own common futures.

Consensus building and NRM in the development context

Some of the principles of ADR and consensus building have been consciously transferred to NRM problem solving in the developing world. The subtlety and level of sophistication of these approaches has increased over time to reflect changes in donor and government development objectives.

Initially, consensus-building principles were seen as a tool to overcome resistance to project-proscribed management, remove the resultant conflict and get project activities back on track. For instance, *alternative conflict resolution* (ACR) as promoted by the IUCN in the early 1990s attempted to build consensus by emphasizing dialogue and developing an improved understanding of the underlying interests of relevant stakeholders. These are basic principles of consensus building and are applied here to smooth the implementation of NRM development projects. However, the criteria for good consensus building processes (Box 1.1) suggest a potentially more subtle contribution to the development process. It is unlikely that early attempts at negotiation and mediation by wildlife conservation staff, for instance, would have resulted in mutual learning between local stakeholders and the convenors of the process. While the principles of consensus building for conservation projects outlined by Borrini-Feyerabend (1997) are sound, if initiatives are externally driven there is a real danger that mediators define the 'acceptable' outcomes, themselves.

There are limits to simply transplanting Western ADR models to the development context, however. The key theme of ADR is one of pro-active engagement and the concerted effort of all parties to seek an agreement. In some respect, the quality of the process will reflect the participants' understanding of ADR (their rights, knowledge of procedure etc.) and the ability

Box 1.1   Criteria for the evaluation of consensus-building processes

Given the range of consensus-related approaches, and their ultimate objectives, the evaluation of their performance can be problematic. However, it is possible to derive indicators of good consensus building from the theoretical- and practice-based literature. Criteria like those below can test the capacity to provide sustained benefits through flexible and adaptive relationships between the stakeholders and, crucially, help gauge the way activities are perceived by the participants themselves.

In sequence, relating to most step-wise processes of consensus building, suitable indicators may include:

- *a shared and common purpose* – although goals may be different, participants must share a common understanding of why they are involved in the process.
- *full participation* – the process should not be controlled by the most vocal or politically powerful.
- *being perceived as fair* – participants should view the process as transparent and balanced.
- *creating a mutual understanding of goals* – participants grow to respect the problems of others and the interconnectedness of local activities (or livelihoods).
- *informing, engaging and interesting participants* – the process should be enlightening and should build awareness.
- *providing inclusive solutions* – ideas and suggestions accommodate as wide a range of stakeholders as possible.
- *encouraging challenges to the status quo* – ideas and suggestions are novel and creative.
- *being self-organizing* – the agenda for debate is selected independently and evolves with time rather than being fixed and imposed by external actors.

[after Innes (2000), Burgess and Burgess (1996) and Kaner (1996).]

of the participants to maintain momentum and dialogue. Any imbalance in skills, knowledge or confidence is likely to weaken the likelihood of reaching lasting consensus. The ability of ADR-type approaches to overcome the power imbalances that characterize much conflict in the developing world is debatable and this problem is not likely to be simply overcome. If disenfranchised groups (landless, women or marginalized ethnic groupings, for instance) are actively supported there is a danger of creating 'coerced harmony' that ultimately works to perpetuate underlying problems (Scialabba, 1998). In addition, ADR requires considerable institutional and financial support and if simple and practical approaches are not adopted, the poor are likely to face high opportunity costs (investments of time) that might discourage participation.

Power issues will also permeate civil society or DIPs attempts to build consensus and reach agreement in the developing world. Whereas DIPs in the developed world may allow direct links to policy formation, similar processes in the developing world tend to extract information for deliberation by policymakers in isolation.[3]

Despite these constraints, there are two important areas where consensus-building principles have been applied to NRM in the development context: understanding and improving the process of planning and co-learning; and improving the management of initiatives to avoid new conflict.

Agricultural knowledge and information systems and platforms for negotiation – an approach to help understand and improve planning and co-learning

Analysis of the process of rural development and extension can take as its starting point the diversity of stakeholder perspectives and the speed of change in their relations and positions. The agricultural knowledge and information systems (AKIS) approach developed by Röling (1992) and others at Wageningen Agricultural University in the Netherlands, rejects a simplistic target-group mentality to extension and places the onus on improved understanding of the role of social institutions in dissemination and learning.[4]

AKIS focuses on the precursors to social innovation for successful agricultural development and stresses that suitable institutions and patterns of interaction must be fostered to reach 'strategic consensus' (Engel and Salomon, 1997). AKIS attempts to build a better understanding of local systems of linkages, the processes of convergence (the merging of positions and ways of thinking) and acknowledges that co-learning is required wherever the complexity and speed of social or environmental change creates conflict. This focus on the convergence of positions in agricultural extension reflects the diversity of objectives, perspectives and relationships within NRM generally, clearly reflecting the principles of consensus building.

The AKIS work on agricultural extension has highlighted four determinants for success within management systems: (1) cooperation between stakeholders; (2) effective communication and information flows; (3) transparency and agreement among stakeholders with respect to interests and objectives; and (4) the proper division and coordination of tasks. To achieve these four determinants, the various stakeholders must be assured access to suitable 'platforms for resource use negotiation' – taken here to mean formal or informal decision-making institutions.[5] These platforms provide the opportunity for social learning by breaking down barriers and encouraging new relations – in turn, increasing the likelihood of creative solutions to NRM problems through collective action rather than positional self-interest.

An important achievement of AKIS has been to elicit a discussion of proper representation and how it is influenced by factors such as stakeholder heterogeneity. Cultural norms should obviously be considered in relation to the role of women or ethnic groups in platforms but it is obviously crucial to include minority interests and perspectives if politically feasible. The relationship between stakeholder diversity and consensual management is not a clear one, however. While it may be assumed that increasing heterogeneity may reduce prospects for consensus and collective decision making, Steins and Edwards (1998), quoting Keohane and Ostrom (1995), suggest that diversity within platforms can add value to processes through the range of insights and skills on offer.

Engel and Salomon (1997) have developed a participatory method that allows extension practitioners and local stakeholders to jointly identify the potential for development through platforms. Rapid Appraisal of Agricultural Knowledge Systems (RAAKS) is a set of tools that seeks to evaluate and understand both the nature of cooperation and conflict and the characteristics of existing institutions and linkages.

There is potential for RAAKS to be applied to scenarios other than those of agricultural extension or the developing world, however, and Engel and Salomon suggest these tools can be applied to any system where the speed of environmental or economic change requires innovative responses. Convergence as the narrowing of 'schools of thought' is analogous to consensus and the AKIS approach represents consensus building for NRM in a useful way. In confronting institutional issues such as the effects of scale, breadth of representation, the role of social learning and informal networks, for instance, it resonates with the sustainable livelihoods approach to development and particularly with respect to the role of social capital, policies, institutions and processes. Crucially, AKIS acknowledges that new platforms do not operate in isolation but are shaped and made useful (or redundant) by the institutional environment in which they sit. The importance of a full understanding of the informal institutional setting is returned to in Chapter 2.

'Managing Conflict and Building Consensus in Rural Livelihoods Projects' – an approach to avoid or manage conflict within initiatives

Warner (1999) has developed a manual for the improved management of participatory community-based and externally driven projects. 'Managing Conflict and Building Consensus in Rural Livelihoods Projects – strategies, principles, tools and training materials' (MCBC) is a comprehensive introduction to consensus building for GOs, NGOs and community partners that outlines the motivation behind conflict and some basic ground rules for seeking consensus.[6]

The aim of MCBC is to improve the management of stakeholder negotiation within NRM projects by highlighting and making accessible the key concepts of consensus building to project managers and personnel. MCBC is careful to approach consensus building as a conflict management tool, recognizing that the goal is not necessarily to remove or tackle the underlying causes of disputes, as conflict resolution does, but to seek 'creative lateral solutions' which supersede the causes of dispute through mutual learning.

In presenting consensus building in the context of the sustainable livelihoods framework and livelihoods assets, Warner suggests a potentially wider role for its application. Consensus building is approached here as a method to improve cooperation and coordination between (and within) civil society and formal institutions. Within the context of the sustainable livelihoods approach, this is achieved by consolidating human capital (through improving skills and awareness-building) and particularly social capital by building trust, fostering open dialogue and creating communication networks between stakeholders. In turn, consensus can both enhance the performance of existing management institutions and lead to the evolution of new institutions or processes.

In addition to consolidating social capital at the local or household level, the manual also presents consensus building as a tool to strengthen vertical linkages between civil society and formal institutions and as a method to strengthen cross-sectoral horizontal linkages between these institutions. In this way, consensus building may have a role to play in improving coordination and integration at the regional and national administrative level.

Consensus building has attracted such interest, Warner argues, because conventional 'adversarial' approaches to conflict have failed to recognize the complexity of local realities. The design of NRM projects in the developing world has tended to restrict opportunities for finding creative solutions to conflict because stakeholder motivation is generally only considered in relation to successful project management and the attainment of project goals set by external agencies. If a 'blueprint' approach is adopted and project design is rigid, the prospects for reaching constructive solutions to underlying conflict are immediately reduced. Although projects may attempt an early understanding of existing conflict and power structures, stakeholder analysis tends to be adopted as a means only to identify beneficiary groups and those groups that provide a threat to achieving project goals. A fundamental understanding of the pattern of interaction between stakeholders and the underlying motives of the parties is not normally considered. Warner presents this as the compromise approach to projects whereby stakeholder analysis uncovers initial positions and then works to find best-fit solutions within the rigid frame of the project. The next requirement in this cycle is to invest time and energy convincing stakeholder groups of the merits of these 'solutions'.

By contrast, a consensus approach first attempts to understand the social and economic needs that shape stakeholders' positions and takes a process approach to project management. In this respect, the MCBC's strategy for consensus building is based on Fisher and Ury's (1981) distinction between positions and interests. Warner states:

> The approach assumes that different stakeholders will find that they have more underlying needs in common than they did initial objectives. This widening of the area of the 'common ground' provides greater scope for finding 'win–win' solutions.

The MCBC approach to consensus building depends on: (1) directing conflicting parties towards addressing their underlying needs and away from negotiating their immediate demands; (2) considering a wide and creative range of options instead of single solutions; and (3) eschewing personalized and exaggerated positions within the conflict and attempting an improved understanding of people's underlying needs.

One advantage of consensus building over an extractive stakeholder analysis approach to project management is that participants are more likely to perceive outcomes as legitimate and useful – participants will perceive a high degree of ownership of the process and of the outcomes which emerge. Warner presents the consensus-building process with respect to ten overlapping stages to be considered in sequence (Figure 1.3). Cultural features relating to the perception of the participants and convenor are acknowledged before a wide range of options are discussed and agreements finally tested.

Figure 1.3 The MCBC principles presented as a step-wise process (Warner, 1999).

In summary, MCBC offers guidance on problem solving within existing projects where there are disputes between project stakeholders, rather than a tool for participatory consensus building prior to specific interventions.

However, incorporating a livelihoods approach and proper awareness of social and political capital opens up a rather more subtle role for consensus building and one which is not merely a response to pre-existing conflict or problems within projects. Rather than a cyclical process of problem identification, brainstorming, problem solving, testing and so on, consensus building might be better expressed as way to create and sustain value through the development of rights or 'access to voice' through social and political capital.

The methods outlined above represent an evolution over several decades in the application of and approach to consensus building. The principles of successful consensus building, originally devised for the civil or corporate setting in the developed world, have remained largely unchanged but new tools have been adopted to provide rounded approaches for use in the developing world context. In particular, the increasing emphasis on stakeholder participation in development has produced tools and methods well suited to creating dialogue and inclusive debate. The common theme of these methods is the emphasis on promoting open channels of communication between stakeholders and mediators and the attempt to understand people's underlying needs and interests rather than attempting to reconcile positions. The relationships and commonalities between the methods are outlined in Table 1.1.

In addition to directed and facilitated consensus building, other significant processes are likely to operate at the local level. There is now a greater awareness of pre-existing and endogenous forms of NRM dispute resolution and

Table 1.1   The origins and purpose of the consensus-building methodologies

Approach	Context	Purpose	Influences	Author
Alternative dispute resolution	Developed world, civic, environmental or planning disputes	Court avoidance, conflict resolution	Anthropological studies of North American and African tribal systems (Gibbs, 1963; Danzig, 1973), US peace movement	Numerous but crystallized by Fisher and Ury (1981)
Future search	Developed world, community or organizational change.	Empower groups to develop action plans to achieve an improved 'future'.	Search Conference (Emery and Trist, 1973), large-scale community futures conferences (Schindler-Rainman and Lippitt, 1980), Participative Strategic Planning Conferences (Jacobs, 1994).	Weisbord and Janoff (1995)
Agricultural knowledge and information systems	Principally agricultural extension in the developing world	Promotion of adaptable and synergistic networks for agricultural development	Theory of Communicative Action (Habermas, 1984), Social Actor Approach (Long and Long, 1992)	Röling (1992), Engel and Salomon (1997)
Managing conflict and building consensus	Community-based NRM projects in the developing world	Successful management of projects (training of project staff)	Sustainable Livelihoods Approach (see Carney, 1999), ADR, Warner (1999)	Fisher and Ury (1981), Moore (1996)

development stakeholders are beginning to acknowledge and understand the role played by these customary processes.

Traditional and modern approaches to consensus building in the developing world

Conflict resolution and consensus building in the developing world tends to draw on combinations of both informal indigenous processes, and formal legal structures of the state. Although these indigenous forms of consensus building may not relate directly to the conceptual approaches outlined above, Moore (1996) has remarked how closely they resemble mediation processes applied in the developed world and Castro (1996) has attempted a classification with respect to their resemblance to negotiation, mediation and arbitration. However, the complex ways in which traditional approaches and customary legal orders are subsumed within local and national legal structures make it difficult to identify typical developing world approaches. It is also inappropriate to present 'modern' Western approaches and 'traditional' indigenous approaches as discrete entities. Castro suggests indigenous approaches should be considered dynamic and evolving, rather than fixed and rigid:

> *Indigenous knowledge does not provide a set formula for community decision-making. It is simply a repertoire of ideas and actions from which individuals and communities faced with specific problems can draw, depending on their own level of knowledge, their preferences, and their ability and motivation to act.*

(Castro, 1996)

Castro considers the structure of conflict resolution in the developing world as one of legal pluralism, whereby the individual, group or community may rely on processes directed by state, religious, ethnic, caste or local systems. In reality these systems overlap, although community members may hold very different views of legitimate authority and decision making from those representing government.

Indigenous conflict resolution at the local level tends to rely on processes of negotiation, mediation and arbitration but a common theme of these approaches is a reliance on face-to-face communication. Cohn (1967) describes how in northern India the first step of simply talking to the other party provides a key function of relieving aggression before entering into negotiation. Once a decision has been reached through mutual agreement or some form of arbitration, then peer pressure, social ostracism or threat may be applied to ensure compliance.

Governments that seek to decentralize legal processes may sometimes set up local procedures and structures for local dispute resolution that draw from indigenous approaches. However, there is a danger here that indigenous and locally respected approaches are co-opted by the state and by the elite to consolidate political structures and maintain current imbalances of power as can happen with the *salish* courts in Bangladesh and the *gram panchayat* in India.

Deliberate attempts to accommodate and recognize traditional practice and customary legal orders within a formal legal structure require a comprehensive understanding of the cultural and political role of these practices and of their suitability within a national system of conflict resolution.[7] There is a danger that indigenous approaches to consensus building are presented as egalitarian processes that necessarily provide fair and equitable outcomes (Nader, 1995). As in all resolution processes, some groups will be better placed to manipulate proceedings through their better knowledge of process or their status. However, it appears that it may be possible to democratize traditional consensus-building methods through the cross-fertilization of developed and developing world approaches.

Transplanting approaches to consensus building

Theoretical and practical approaches to conflict management and consensus building have tended to understate the diversity of perceptions, norms and values that shape the cultural context of conflict and negotiation. Because these approaches are predominantly designed in response to disputes in the developed world (particularly the USA) they often lack what Kramer and Messick (1995) term a 'social contextualist perspective'. In other words, much of the theory and practice of consensus building is too generic, often failing to consider the local significance of conflict and consensus and how local actors react to facilitation or perceive compromise, for instance. As Rabbie (1994) states:

> *The importance of culture and cultural symbols in facilitating or hindering cross-cultural communications dictates a need to incorporate cultural attitudes and perceptions into models and theories of conflict analysis and conflict resolution. Models that were produced by Western specialists have continued to lack the proper tools to deal with non-Western nations, and thus they have remained largely irrelevant to those people.*

This theme has been taken up repeatedly, particularly with respect to conflict resolution and the transplantation of developed world approaches elsewhere. Miall et al. (1999) acknowledge that adapting theory and practice between cultural contexts is the most pressing and challenging task facing the field of conflict resolution. However, the approach to researching conflict and consensus in the developed world has focussed on the attainment of measurable outcomes and products (such as civil dispute settlements, court avoidance etc.) rather than the processes themselves in a social context (Thompson et al., 1995). This focus may not be universally appropriate, though. In describing the complex and apparently unpredictable interaction between social and physical systems, Uphoff (1996) suggests that a typically Eastern 'both/and' worldview that acknowledges the overlapping, interactive nature of systems may be more appropriate than social science based on a Western 'either/or' epistemology.[8] Non-Western cultures often adopt a creative and inclusive stance to conflict (a non-zero-sum perspective) and this cooperative approach can contribute to the development of conflict resolution in the West.[9]

Lund et al. (1994) emphasize that models should not be interventionist but culture-centred, incorporating culturally sensitive assessments of each scenario and, presumably, applying suitable participatory tools and approaches. Such an assessment would have to consider the cultural context of conflict and local norms of negotiation.[10]

Although this cultural diversity in the perception of conflict and consensus is widely acknowledged, anthropological models may be limited in offering pragmatic solutions to adapting existing approaches. A livelihoods perspective might provide a framework with which to better gauge the relevance of different approaches to building consensus.

Consensus building within a livelihoods perspective

Consensus building can be viewed as both: (1) a directed attempt to promote collective action through mutual learning and the development of appropriate stakeholder institutions; or (2) a means to better achieve *other* project or programme goals through a holistic and participatory approach to design and management. Both scenarios fit well with the sustainable livelihoods framework as outlined by Carney (1999) and DFID (2000).

Through building or reinforcing horizontal relationships, trust and reciprocity within the community and vertical links with other groups and institutions, consensus building obviously relates to social capital.

There are a number of parallels between current concepts of social capital and concepts relating to consensus. Krishna and Shrader (1999), for instance, have developed a framework that distinguishes between two forms of local social capital, *cognitive* and *structural*. Cognitive social capital refers to shared values, beliefs, attitudes, social norms and the tendency to cooperate. According to Krishna and Shrader, it represents 'the trust, solidarity and reciprocity that are shared amongst members of a community and that can create conditions under which communities can work together for a common good'. Structural social capital includes the composition and practices of formal and informal local institutions that serve as instruments of community development. This can be developed with the right platforms. 'Structural social capital is built through horizontal organizations and networks that have collective and transparent decision making processes, accountable leaders, and practices of collective action and mutual responsibility'. These structures are most likely to emerge in situations where higher levels of cognitive social capital already exist, however.

This differentiation between existing, cultural components of social capital and that which surrounds institutional structures would appear useful with respect to strategizing approaches to consensus building.

Similarly, mutual learning through participation and the sharing of knowledge will enhance human capital by developing new skills, a greater understanding of livelihoods options and an awareness of new approaches to decision making and dispute resolution.

Building consensus can have a subtle role in helping to provide options for the poor and socially excluded. Greater attention is now being directed to the environment of policies, institutions and processes (PIPs) that surrounds the poor and which ultimately shapes access to the benefits derived from natural resources and other assets. In Bangladesh, for instance, many of the problems of fulltime fishers relate to these types of transforming processes (Barr et al., 2000). Frequently, de facto access arrangements and the difficulties of enforcing de jure property rights mean that fishers are unable to convert their environmental endowments into entitlements (Leach et al., 1997).[11] By building consensus, fishers could gain sufficient social capital to be able to withstand or challenge discriminatory local practices.

The consensus-building process, then, acts at the interface between people's assets and livelihood options. Any new networks of communication and formal or informal institutions for decision making that result can bring new opportunities for the poor with them. In summary, consensus and social capital can help people explore new livelihood options. These options may relate to new forms of production and to natural resources or might extend to other aspects of rural development, marketing and planning.

There are parallels between the sustainable livelihoods framework generally (a focus on participation, an awareness of the interconnectedness of stakeholders and their actions, the need to strengthen the capacity to deal with shocks and trends) and effective consensus building. In relation to consensus in NRM, for instance, if processes are externally driven there is a danger of overlooking very site specific social, economic and environmental characteristics that are essential to understanding ongoing disputes. It is crucial that participatory approaches to consensus building should be adopted (by NGOs, government agencies, community groups etc.) if the comparative advantage of locally appropriate strategies and endogenous skills and knowledge are not to be overlooked. The approaches and lessons learned from conflict management elsewhere will contribute, but local stakeholders must play a central role in creating new relations and platforms for action.

There is little doubt that the ability (or inability) to access political influence plays a central role in shaping people's options and, ultimately, their livelihoods.[12] It is possible that some types of consensus building can develop or utilize political capital by reinvigorating pre-existing but under-used government structures and service providers. Participatory planning can create a unified demand for targeted assistance and place a new emphasis on those stakeholders mandated to deliver development support.

The rest of the book focuses on this next step and how the consensus-building tool PAPD has helped build new political and institutional linkages for isolated communities.

Participatory Action Plan Development (PAPD)

PAPD attempts to combine some of the generic principles for consensus-building practice with a range of tools and approaches that have been applied within participatory rural appraisal (PRA) over the last two decades.

The methodology evolved from research on the livelihoods of the poor in floodplain Bangladesh conducted principally by Julian Barr of the Centre for Land Use and Water Resources at the University of Newcastle and Peter Dixon at the University of Durham in the UK, and Mokhlesur Rahman and Anisul Islam at the Centre for Natural Resource Studies (CNRS) in Dhaka.[13] Building on an approach to uncover and report the livelihoods constraints faced by the range of floodplain stakeholders (Barr et al., 2000), the methodology was developed and tested as a structured workshop process specifically intended to build trust and social capital through planning. PAPD has since been used in several large NRM projects throughout Bangladesh and in Vietnam and India.

PAPD is centred on:

- a recognition of the range and connectedness of livelihood interests within 'communities';
- acknowledgment of the role of social capital and institutional support in collective action;

- an understanding of group dynamics and the value of a well-facilitated and punctuated sequence of tasks and achievements; and
- the use of simple participatory tools with participants.

Fundamental to the PAPD approach is its acknowledgement of the limits of viewing the 'community' as a heterogeneous and harmonious entity. The common property resource (CPR) literature has too often assumed a simple link between local community management, the ability to take collective action, and sustainability in NRM. However, a livelihoods perspective has encouraged researchers and development practitioners to look beyond simplistic notions of the community as groups static in time and space and to consider the diversity of interests, linkages and power relations that might influence options for poverty alleviation and sustainability. PAPD acknowledges that 'recognising and working with the multiplicity of actors and interests is crucial for those advocating community-based programmes' (Agrawal and Gibson, 1999).

In this setting, then, consensus building requires an increased understanding of this complexity by the facilitator *and* by local stakeholders.

The PAPD process recognizes the parallels between social capital and concepts of consensus and attempts to raise awareness of the diversity of local concerns and interests in order to develop empathy between groups before moving towards mutually acceptable and potential win–win activities. Political representatives and government service providers are included at strategic points in the planning process to build vertical linkages, ensure future support and to increase the perceived legitimacy of discussion and resulting plans.

Drawing from consensus-building approaches in the Western context, PAPD adopts a highly structured sequence intended to focus the attention of participants on potential mutual gains and to avoid re-visiting well-rehearsed recriminations and positions in public. Kaner (1996) highlights how the quality of discussion during unstructured public planning tends to decline leaving the participants confused and unable to reach consensus – 'business as usual'. According to Kaner, skilfully facilitated processes are crucial and participants must have a shared frame of reference and a good understanding of why they are involved in discussion. Facilitators must help ensure that the natural process of *divergence* is punctuated by interventions or activities that keep the discussion grounded and on a path towards potential agreement through *convergence*. As with Future Search, the real prospect of change during PAPD – in this case, a locally implemented plan to solve a NRM problem – enables participants to focus on ideal envisioned futures that might accommodate all interests.

PAPD applies several approaches and tools considered good practice in rural appraisal. These include the careful facilitation of groups to prevent intimidation of the less vocal and the use of visual and easily understood activities such as problem census and resource mapping (see below).

In summary, PAPD is intended as a methodology to build local consensus by uncovering co-dependencies and developing greater understanding between stakeholders. It is also meant to highlight opportunities to facilitators and options for future management, especially in a project context.

The PAPD methodology in detail

The overall theme of PAPD is to stress that problem solving may result in unexpected outcomes and new opportunities. This is, in part, because the problems themselves are not pre-determined by the facilitator but are the output of joint discussion. The aim of PAPD is to develop agreement and collective action on future management strategies that address the needs of all groups and their interests.

The normal sequence of PAPD activities elaborated by Barr and Dixon (2001) is outlined in Figure 1.4. There are three basic phases:

(1) a scoping phase which attempts to uncover local institutional issues and identify key participants through stakeholder analysis;
(2) a participatory planning phase which comprises the workshop proper and uncovers key issues and potential solutions; and finally
(3) an implementation phase in which agreements are converted into action through appropriate management and institutional design.

Stage 1: Situation analysis, reconnaissance social survey and stakeholder analysis

Situation analysis is conducted by the facilitating agency in order to gain an insight into locale-specific community and NRM issues. This process may involve the triangulation of feedback from key informants in a social survey but PAPD has often been applied in contexts where the facilitator already has local knowledge and has established a good understanding and rapport with local people.

Stakeholder analysis deconstructs the 'community' and acknowledges that distinct groups exist with differing (but overlapping) livelihood concerns and interests. The aim is to represent the diversity of these interests within the workshops and a micro-census may be used to categorize village households by broad grouping. Normally, about five groups are identified and 15–20 households from each grouping are invited to attend the workshop stage of PAPD.

Stage 2: Problems census, problem clustering and planning workshops

Stages 2 and 3 are workshop-based and in total take about five to eight days to complete. The initial stage of the PAPD workshop centres on a problem census held with each stakeholder group in isolation. The participants list and rank problems that impact their livelihoods, together with tentative solutions for NRM-related problems. The prioritized problems tend to relate to repeated underlying causes. The facilitators attempt to 'cluster' these problems and to ensure those issues affecting the most poor and vulnerable are taken forward.

The planning workshops constitute three sessions. First, the core problems are discussed in plenary to encourage debate on inter-dependencies between the groups before a series of matrices are completed by each group over a period of several days. Participants are encouraged to think of the consequences of the problems and any proposed solutions across the range of local stakeholders. A key activity at this stage is STEPS analysis that examines social, technical, environmental, political and sustainability issues for each proposal in detail.

For instance, all participants are encouraged to identify what social issues must be considered (how different groups might be affected positively or negatively) and what arrangements might be required to minimize potential problems.

Finally, facilitators collate the contributions of the groups before their efforts are presented in plenary. The objective here is to focus on commonalities between the concerns and interests of all stakeholders. Open floor discussion functions to resolve any remaining misunderstandings and the desired end point is broad agreement on the *type* of intervention to pursue for maximum benefit.

Stage 3: Development of implementing institutions and implementation of plan

This stage begins with initial discussion of the structure, membership and function of any committee or group entrusted to coordinate the implementation of the action plan. The STEPS analysis provides a basis for the allocation of roles and responsibilities such as financing, technical expertise and support and linkage to local government. By this stage, the presence of local government representatives and fisheries or agriculture service providers during plenary sessions should have helped to forge the necessary linkages.

The overall intention is that local consensus, focussed on a useful public initiative, can create new social and institutional linkages, opening up new opportunities for the vulnerable and highlighting the potential benefits of inclusion and collaboration.

PAPD has generally been applied in the context of large NRM projects and the design of this committee and its intended linkage to other institutions may reflect existing project structures. The implementation of plans may run parallel to other project activities or may occur after project end. In either case, PAPD provides a systematic methodology to attract community support and to quickly identify unifying interventions. More importantly, the approach provides a foothold for longer-term resource-use negotiation, committee formation and community-based management. Because PAPD is applied in the project context, implemented activities are intended to fit overall project themes and objectives – in the case of Bangladesh, this is commonly the sustainable management of fisheries and floodplain resources via local community-based organizations.

Several of the resource-use dilemmas and conflicts surrounding aquatic resources are common throughout rural Bangladesh, as are the potential solutions. For instance, CNRS have found that waterbody or canal re-excavation can often unite communities because increased water flow improves fisheries (inward movement of stocks and breeding fish) and farming interests (increased irrigable water and reduced stagnation) simultaneously.

CNRS now has considerable experience of applying the PAPD workshop approach in a focussed and directed manner in the project setting. The organization has worked within the fisheries, agriculture and water sectors with both NGO and government partners and continues to promote the methodology within and outside Bangladesh.[14]

Finally, there are indications that PAPD has potential applications in contexts other than local community planning. The University of Stirling in the UK and the West Bengal Department of Environment in India have tested the PAPD

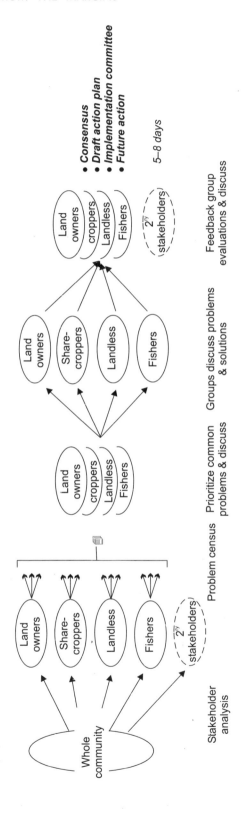

Figure 1.4 The PAPD method for consensus building. PAPD is workshop-based and takes approximately eight days to conduct. The stakeholder groups presented here are typical of those in the Bangladesh floodplain (after Barr & Dixon, 2001).

principles in the East Kolkata wetlands with its diverse array of poor, business and government interest groups (see Bunting, 2006). Pilot water-management initiatives were identified by helping primary stakeholders articulate their needs with service providers through a series of separate and open workshops. The planning process here was intended to mirror the various stages of group discussion, plenary, modification etc. of PAPD but applied across several geographic and administrative levels.

Synthesis – a typology of consensus building in NRM

In summary, consensus-building processes in the context of NRM may be applied (or entered into by participants) for a variety of reasons. The typology in Table 1.3 attempts to illustrate the basic range of consensus-building methods and their functions. The pupose of consensus building will influence the design, character and approach so that methodologies may adopt either fixed or flexible structures to problem solving or problem identification. From left to right, the typology represents a gradient from directed trouble shooting – where the goal of consensus building may be pre-defined and the character and outcomes of process may largely be dictated by a third party – to facilitated and participatory processes where problem identifiction may play as central a role as problem solving itself. Culturally specific and informal approaches to building consensus in NRM are acknowledged (shown shaded in the table), but the focus is on those processes where efforts are in some way initiated, managed or supported by an external third party.

Type A – Establishment of NRM initiatives

This form of intervention assumes a constraint to some pre-defined management objective. Consensus building in this context is perceived as a method to remove the constraint and to achieve given management or project goals. However, because the underlying causes of management problems (what motivates stakeholders, institutional constraints etc.) may remain unknown, the third party may need to rely on enforcement or repeated interventions to implement change. Borrini-Feyerabend et al. (2000), for example, acknowledge that many past attempts to achieve nature conservation targets had relied on top-down and rigid approaches to problem solving. More recent approaches have attempted to incorporate participatory methods and a wider community and livelihoods perspective. These types of process may also use educational campaigns and awareness building to strengthen local support.

Example

Gujja et al. (1998) have applied a participatory and consultative approach to assist project design for the improved management of the Ucchali wetlands of Pakistan. It was acknowledged that the current integrated management plan for the region had created tensions between the various user groups and the agencies responsible for the area's management. A process of discussion between

Table 1.2 The four basic NRM consensus-building 'types' with respect to purpose, character and effect

CB Purpose	Type A	Type B	Type C	Type D
	Establishment of NRM initiatives	Problem solving within NRM initiatives	Promotion of mutually beneficial collective action	Local processes to create consensus and avoid conflict (sustain social capital)
Example	ACR to achieve 'collaborative management' of wildlife projects	Alternative conflict management to remove obstacles to successful implementation	PAPD to identify problems and reach envisioned futures	Local dispute resolution
Character of process	Pursuit of sectoral / agency objectives	Balancing multiple stakeholder objectives	Mutual learning and inclusive planning	Traditional or existing approaches
	Arbitration by external agency	Mediation by external agency	Facilitation with external agency	Facilitation, mediation or arbitration
Outcome	Short-term objectives met/ underlying conflict may remain/enforce-ment may be required	Trade-offs negotiated and project strategy achieved/ consensus is project specific/ change may not outlive project	Social capital and decision making supported/ gains intended to outlive facilitation	Status quo maintained
Example	Community-based planning for wetland management, Pakistan (Gujja et al., 1998)	Framework for consensus participation in protected areas, Zambia (Warner, 1997)	Participatory Action Plan Development at Posna, Diksi and Kathuria, Bangladesh	Arbitration by *mathbor* of *salish* courts, Bangladesh (Center for Democracy and Governance, 2000)

and within a range of stakeholder groups was initiated to breakdown the adversarial relationship and to identify mutually acceptable proposals with local communities. The facilitators provided an educational role in assessing and explaining the feasibility and potential impacts of the suggested management strategies. However, in this example of 'collaborative management', the boundaries that define acceptable or inappropriate management suggestions and scenarios were essentially pre-defined by national and international obligations under the Ramsar Convention.[15]

Type B – Problem solving within NRM initiatives

This form of process acknowledges the diversity of stakeholders, their interests and motivations. There is a concerted attempt to understand the positions taken by individuals or groups and to create new and more productive lines of discussion and debate. The third party acts as mediator by guiding and encouraging interaction between the parties and there is a horizontal process of dialogue between local stakeholders. The process is designed to improve the impact and effectiveness of ongoing projects or programmes and may be either reactive to problems as they arise (a form of troubleshooting to redirect the project) or may draw on pre-designed and project-specific institutions as 'platforms' for negotiation. In both cases, the process may be a cyclical one of negotiation, adaptation, monitoring, negotiation and so on.

Although the type of problems may not be pre-empted by the mediator (as in Type A processes), the design of the consultation process, the role of local stakeholders, and their subsequent role in the project more generally, is largely dictated by the third party concerned.

Example

The 'Framework for Consensus Participation in Protected Areas' (FCPPA) provides step-wise guidance for undertaking participatory and consensus-seeking negotiations for project planning or management (Warner, 1997). The FCPPA was developed and tested in the setting of Game Management Areas in Zambia and was a directed attempt to improve participation in the design of management plans. The process centres on several distinct activities that represent stakeholder analysis and assessment, participatory community assessment, and finally, planning and participatory monitoring and evaluation. Warner suggests that the FCPPA can perform either of two functions – to help design new conservation and development projects or to shape periodic strategic exercises within ongoing projects.

At each of the steps the facilitating agency has a central role in identifying, assessing and guiding stakeholders, and although Warner recommends adopting impartial (non-wildlife authority) personnel, the outcomes and scope of the process must, by definition, be a conservation-oriented one.

Type C – Promotion of mutually beneficial collective action

This type of process does not search for discrete solutions to single, identifiable problems but emphasizes the value of new stakeholder interactions and mutual learning through facilitated discussion. Although collective action might be promoted, it is the reinforcement of social capital that is intended to benefit communities, both within and outside the sphere of projects or programmes. In this respect, the design and application of this type of process is not exclusive to project management and does not presume identifiable technical constraints to development.

Example

The PAPD process introduces the key issues faced by each stakeholder group to all participants with an emphasis on highlighting commonalities between people's interests and how potential solutions might accommodate all concerns. In this regard, much depends on the expertise of facilitators in guiding and motivating participants towards successful and constructive outcomes.

PAPD was first piloted in Bangladesh at three seasonal *beels* (shallow lakes) with promising results and with broad local approval (Barr and Dixon, 2001). Stakeholders identified a wide range of problems relating to agriculture, declining fisheries, the siltation of connecting canals and lack of unity among local people. Summary tables were prepared with the facilitators to help demonstrate the range of problems, alternative solutions and their knock-on effects on different interest groups. At each of the three sites, the facilitators and the participants were able to develop detailed and mutually beneficial plans – potential interventions that supported both farm *and* fisheries livelihoods.[16]

Once a provisional plan was agreed, local government officials were invited to witness plenary sessions and to grant their support. Planning then turned to the role and function of a resource management or implementation committee. The proposed action plans and committee structures were then taken forward to form the basis of subsequent dialogue and management.

PAPD was later adopted as the key planning tool in the national Community-Based Fisheries Management Project (1995–2005) and has since been applied within the water and environment sectors and in the coastal setting of Bangladesh.

The focus on problem identification, rather than problem solving alone, and the development of alternative management scenarios acknowledges Future Search but PAPD also draws on a suite of activities and tools commonly associated with PRA (for instance, problem census, time-lines, diagramming and mapping).

Type D – Local processes to create consensus and avoid conflict

These processes operate at a local scale, either with or without the formal acknowledgement of the state, and tend to function as dispute-resolution mechanisms. Groups or individuals may act as arbiters, mediators or facilitators in cases that may directly or indirectly reflect NRM issues (conflicts over access rights, land disputes etc.). Whether the mechanisms are driven by an underlying motive to maintain the status quo and current power structures, or whether they are concerted attempts to avoid violence, communities tend to draw on a wide array of procedures to treat disputes: avoidance, coercion, negotiation, mediation, arbitration and adjudication (Nader and Todd, 1978).

Example

In Bangladesh, the traditional body for dispute resolution is the *salish* court, comprised of several respected *mathbor* elders (see section 2.3 for a discussion of *salish* in more detail). The process is a directed one, and the various parties are encouraged, with considerable input from the court, to reach consensus.

Although the ability of the *salish* to impose or influence agreements will reflect the local status of its members (rather than an ability to reach equitable or informed decisions), the *salish* of Bangladesh has traditionally represented people of all religions and is accessible to everyone regardless of literacy or status (Center for Democracy and Governance, 2000).

In summary, the approach to consensus building has reflected the objectives of facilitating agencies. Type A processes are akin to problem solving, where issues are identified externally and local stakeholders are consulted in an attempt to modify practice and gain compliance. Type B processes attempt to establish community representation through special committee structures but the scope of planning is still limited by project or agency objectives. Type C processes are intended to explore options with communities in the broad context of NRM or rural development. The social capital and institutional links that may emerge here are considered as important as the visible outcomes and products of planning.

Chapters 2 and 3 focus on experiences with PAPD – a Type C process – in the charlands of Bangladesh. Interestingly, it appears that this approach is strengthened and made more legitimate by the deliberate inclusion of existing informal institutions such as the *salish* and other forms of decision making centred around kinship groups (Type D processes). It seems crucial that facilitated attempts to build consensus develop a complete understanding of existing mechanisms, acknowledge them publicly, and aim to somehow accommodate them.

2

Consensus building in the Bangladesh charlands

Poverty alleviation is about reducing the incidence of poverty via individual processes of graduation and successful incorporation into existing social arrangements and patterns of distribution. Poverty eradication relies upon the principle of structural change, and is about the cohorts of the poor confronting power and inequality.

(Wood, 2003)

This chapter sets out the experience of Practical Action in adapting and testing the PAPD methodology in two char villages in Jamalpur District, Bangladesh. First, a brief overview of the socio–political structure of rural Bangladesh is provided to help illustrate the potential role and challenges for participatory processes like PAPD in poverty eradication. The description of the institutional environment of remote and deprived villages here is intended to help orientate the reader and illustrate the key features of the setting in which the PAPD process was tested.

The process of democratization in late developing countries often takes place in a context where civil society remains weak (Westergaard and Hossein, 2002). This is the case in Bangladesh, a country that is characterized by an absence of strongly organized trade unions, peasant organizations and other civil society groups. For many, participation in the national political process is only achievable through clientelism and the use of vertical patron–client relationships and this can mean that a concern for social justice is often displaced by individualism.

Several commentators have suggested that geographic or bio-physical features of the Bangladesh landscape have worked to shape the livelihood strategies and behaviours that now influence the realpolitik of local decision-making and representation. Islam (2002), for instance, argues that spatial factors may explain the lack of organized civil society groups at local level. Bangladesh has open villages with a dispersed, linear pattern of settlement, different from the close or corporate villages found in other parts of South Asia. The local administrative structure superimposed on this landscape has to function across small clusters of hamlets – *para* – and this may militate against the close local integration of people and a common identity within a local space.

The link between national NGOs and local bureaucratic and political systems such as the Union Parishad (UP) remains weak and there is little evidence of interaction between emerging peoples' organizations or community based organizations (CBOs) developed by NGOs and the representative structures of government (Thornton 2002). Local communities remain dislocated: the village is the 'done to' institution and the UP the unempowered tier of government.

The implicit target for development agencies and NGOs is this formal institutional vacuum at the village level. Unfortunately, interventions normally attempt to ameliorate the symptoms of political marginalization whilst overlooking the informal institutions and processes that operate to either obstruct new initiatives or to enable positive and lasting change.

The informal institutional environment of the poor

In the widest sense, institutions refer to any regularized patterns of behaviour and practice. This definition incorporates not only formal, corporate institutions, but also traditional social institutions and informal relations (after Leach et al., 1997).

Informal institutions (as norms and behaviour) interact with the network of government and non-government structures and shape their performance.[17] This interaction is most manifest at the local level where the role and impact of policy and central government is superimposed by other dynamics and concerns.

Informal institutions strongly influence the distribution of resources and opportunities but are frequently overlooked by NRM facilitators and donors. In the context of Bangladesh, Islam (2002) has discussed how the *samaj* and the *salish*, in particular, dominate people's lives and livelihoods. The *samaj* is a sort of residential brotherhood that permeates society in rural Bangladesh. It represents 'an institutional space for collective worship, performance of rituals and festivals' but its impact and influence is much broader than this. Crucially it represents a mode of social control relying on 'psychological coercion or manipulation according to socially constructed notions of honour and shame.' The *samaj* operates to coordinate activity centred on the mosque, to dictate access to significant social events, to form a bridge for negotiation between external agencies and the local group and to influence voting behaviour (Bertocci, 1996).

The village-level judicial system of *salish* is virtually ubiquitous in rural Bangladesh. Although the *salish* is still frequently used for fast and inexpensive dispute resolution with respected elders (*mathbor*) acting as arbiters, its composition appears to be changing as new strategic actors such as Union Parishad representatives and others with party political interests start to play a greater role (Islam, 2002). However, some NGO facilitators of rural development are now targeting the *salish* as a potential platform for gender-sensitive and egalitarian negotiation.

Some social norms in rural Bangladesh are associated with the allegiance and legitimacy shown within the clan group or *gusthi*. The PAPD experiences outlined later were strongly influenced by the composition of the displaced communities in the villages so that decision making and influence was, to a large extent, retained within *gusthi* and less likely to influence individuals of other clans.

Briefly, the institution of patron–clientism should be acknowledged. While there are obviously complicated relationships between different sections of society based on power, access to resources, labour and favour, Islam (2002) explains how conventional notions of patronage are becoming outmoded. Rather than the traditionally held image of the landlord–peasant (feudal) relationship, there now appears to be a new form of patronage evolving and one which 'is more to do with the penetration of macro-politics into the rural space and people's need for protection against escalating violence'.

Although these informal institutions obviously impinge on NRM issues, either directly or indirectly, they tend to be disregarded or bypassed by development initiatives. With respect to rural development then, pre-existing institutions should not only be acknowledged, but incorporated into policy or project design and approach, rather than bypassed or challenged.

Many of the informal processes that dictate access to resources and options for the poor are remarkably resilient in the face of change. Westergaard and Hossein (1997) have discussed in detail the difficulties of directly challenging exploitative behaviours and patterns of ownership in the floodplains of Bangladesh. Attempts to continue the fight for access to land and water resources have placed a heavy toll on the poor:

> For more than three decades, the ownership status of the land in Beel Kuralia has been disputed: in 1956 the government acquired the land, but this ownership was challenged by the jotedars (rich peasants). Subsequently, many contradictory rulings from different government quarters have been issued; and fighting over the land has caused a lot of hardship, not least to the poor fishermen and farmers in the area. A lot of law suits have been filed, the landless have spent about Tk. 150,000 [approximately US$2,200] on court cases and other expenses for the movement. Besides, the landless have been in and out of jail for years.

(Westergaard and Hossein, 1997)

Developing char-modified PAPD

PAPD was designed to include poor and marginalized social groups in community-level dialogue and negotiation and in this regard it may exceed some simplistic rights-based approaches that highlight democratic or electoral support in isolation from considerations of real power. The PAPD principles are intended to accommodate the local realities of the poor and the complex and stubborn power relationships they currently endure. The process does not represent an immediate threat to influential resource holders and elites. It can be put into operation, for example, within that patron-client setting described by Wood (2003) in which:

> ...poor men and women are dominated by dysfunctional time preference behaviour in which the pursuit of immediately needed security places them in relationships and structures which then displace the longer term prospects of a sustained improvement in their livelihoods.

In summary, PAPD and consensual planning has the potential to uncover novel options for poor groups currently stifled by what CARE Bangladesh (2002) has termed the 'net of power relations'. It does this by encouraging the facilitator to consider this informal institutional environment and together with the community to identify important brokers (individuals, service providers, other local institutions) for pro-poor support and action.

PAPD has predominantly been used for consensus building and planning in the context of the Bangladesh floodplain where it was first developed. Practical Action Bangladesh has since applied and tested the same principles in a very different context whilst working with communities in the northern Bangladesh charlands of the Jamuna River (see Box 2.1).

'Consensus for a holistic approach to improve rural livelihoods in riverine islands of Bangladesh (CHAR)' was an action research project conducted by Practical Action Bangladesh between 2001 and 2004 and supported by the Natural Resources Systems Programme of the UK Department for International Development. Practical Action's Reducing Vulnerability programme focuses on the food security of landless and near landless households and PAPD fits well with Practical Action's existing strategies for raising food production. The project was initiated to explore the modification of the PAPD methodology to the charlands context with a five member multi-disciplinary team of field level research associates supported by senior staff in Dhaka.

A recent priority for Practical Action has been to change the extension process in its food security projects from an 'expert driven' to a 'farmer driven' one. The PAPD methodology was seen as an opportunity for Practical Action to open out its local planning processes and to increase the opportunities for leadership and ownership to emerge from local communities and institutions.

The parallels between PAPD and its focus on problem identification, problem solving and public agreement, and Practical Action's experiences with participatory technology development (PTD) were obvious to the organization. Of particular interest was the way in which the PAPD process might open up new institutional relationships for the poor, moving beyond early technical advances to tackle more intractable social and political issues that are particularly extreme in remote areas such as the charlands.

Box 2.1 Chars and charlands of Bangladesh

A char is an accretion of land in a river course or estuary. Within the continuous process of erosion and accretion in the rivers of Bangladesh, the sandbars emerge as islands within the river channel (island chars) or as attached land to the riverbanks (attached chars), often creating new opportunities for settlement and agriculture. The chars are extremely vulnerable to both erosion and flood hazards. Recent analysis of time series satellite images indicates that over 99 per cent of the area within the banks of the Jamuna River had been char at one time or another between 1973 and 2000. The same analysis shows that about 75 per cent of the chars existed for only one to nine years, while only about 10 per cent lasted for 18 years or more.

(Source: Banglapedia website, http://banglapedia.search.com.bd)

PAPD experience in the floodplain context has illustrated the value of simple and visible, cross-cutting interventions. The strategy there was to demonstrate the potential of consensual planning early on and to try to establish and sustain enthusiasm and participation. The Practical Action team decided to adopt a similar strategy, helping the communities identify and tackle simple and discrete 'low-risk' interventions early on in the process. 'High-risk' issues were only to be attempted when trust and confidence had first been raised through early breakthroughs and successes.

The Practical Action team predicted a strong correlation between the level of conflict generated by an issue and the investment of time and effort required to build consensus. It appeared likely that there would be a trade-off between the impact and popularity of consensus building from having successfully navigated serious and cross-cutting problems and the risks of losing support and credibility through failure. Lower risk interventions associated with technical support were less likely to fail but were also less likely to challenge the social and institutional features of the chars that function to constrain the poor. In summary, Practical Action intended to apply its experience of a range of simple food production technologies to create a positive setting for consensus-building work on more entrenched issues.

The charlands of Bangladesh suffer from several physical and institutional features that compound their remoteness from markets and which severely limit opportunities for poverty alleviation. In this setting, where social capital within displaced communities is lacking and where local conflicts are centred on contested land rights, Practical Action's key PAPD modification was expected to relate to timescale. The issues were not neatly bounded and were unlikely to be resolved quickly in a workshop setting where villagers were unused to interacting with development agencies and political stakeholders.

Some of the key social characteristics of charlands are given in Box 2.2.

The preparatory phase in Nadagari and Nandina

In 2001, Practical Action began piloting PAPD in two villages in the charlands of Jamalapur District, north Bangladesh (photograph 3). The villages were carefully selected to represent the range of physical and social characters of char settlements in the area.

Nadagari village

Established in 1992, the village is relatively young, even in the context of the chars. Nadagari lies seven to eight kilometres from the Madarganj Upazila town and 32 kilometres from Jamalpur district town. There is no road in the village and during the dry season most people walk the seven to eight kilometres to reach Madarganj town, travelling on uneven surfaces and through surface water (photograph 4). A journey to the town entails a ferry journey across a tributary of the Jamuna river.

Box 2.2 Poverty in the Bangladesh charlands

- *Char population*: An estimated seven million people live on the chars and associated flood- and famine-prone areas, approximately 5 per cent of the population of Bangladesh.
- *Seasonal flooding*: Chars may be submerged for over two months of the year. Accumulation of physical assets in these circumstances is extremely difficult (photograph 1).
- *Physical constraints of charlands*: The ephemeral and shifting character of the chars presents particular problems in relation to land ownership and security of access for the poor. The constant accretion and erosion of the charlands mean that land disputes are common.
- *Poor communication*: Road communications are poor or non-existent between charlands and the mainland, constraining the movement of people and goods. Although most char villages can be reached within three hours from the nearest district town, the chars are perceived to be cut off, remote and socially alien by the majority of Bangladeshis. Government services fail to reach the charlands (photograph 2).
- *Distance from government and other formal institutions*: Although government departments are present at Upazila and UP level, government officials rarely visit char areas. Char people have difficulty in accessing essential services of health and education. The absence of banks or government credit systems and the weak service offered by agriculture, livestock and fishery agencies means little assistance is available to enhance people's income or to help protect their assets.
- *Lack of access to health and education*: Char areas are deprived of education and health services. In most places, diseases associated with the normal monsoon cycle are reported to be a greater cause of death than floods. The level of literacy is extremely poor and lags far behind the national average.
- *Poor coverage of NGOs*: National NGOs have little presence in charlands and are only recently showing a greater interest in such marginal areas. NGOs perceive greater logistical constraints and physical and financial risks of working in these areas.
- *Difference between chars in northern and southern regions*: Although chars are subject to regular erosion and flooding, chars located in the northern region of the country are less fertile and generally have a lower population density. There appears to be a lower level of violent conflict in the north as a result.
- *Chronic poverty*: More than 80 per cent of char dwellers earn less than US$1 per day. Out migration is very high and over 60 per cent of households are female headed for most of the year. In villages surveyed by Practical Action, it was found that the majority of households survive on 10 to 15 cents per day. In other words they are below the international poverty line by a factor of ten.

The village is about 16 km² with up to about 8,800 people resident over the year (1,960 households). Typical of isolated chars that emerge from the river bed, the soil is sandy and nutrient poor. Rice, millet, chilli, potato and groundnuts are the most widely grown crops and agriculture engages the majority of the villagers as sharecroppers or labourers. The village has no market, doctor, medical shop or dispensary and people depend on the local *kabiraj* (traditional healer) for healthcare. The majority of Nadagari's residents are illiterate and there is one primary school in the village.

Photo 1   A family marooned during the 2004 flood

Photo 2   Char residents crossing a river channel on the way to market

Photo 3   The Practical Action team crossing to Nadagari village

Nandina village

Nandina is a medium-sized char village that has been in existence for about fifty years. The village is classified an attached char because it is separated from

Photo 4   Char Nadagari in the dry season

the mainland by only a single seasonal channel. It lies fifteen kilometres from Sarishabari town but the village is not easily accessible. Travelling to the town requires a three kilometre walk to the metalled Sarishabari road and during the rainy season the journey must be undertaken by boat. The village has a small market but for most needs villagers travel to the Shaymganj-Kalibari market eighteen kilometres away. As with Nadagari, there is no electricity in the village and only the most privileged have sanitary latrines. In 2004 there was a total of about 3,500 permanent and seasonal residents in the village (approximately 600 households). The majority are landless households involved in agriculture-related activities, sometimes supplemented with trading and fishing activity. A large number of residents migrate to the towns for seasonal employment opportunities. Two waterbodies provide some private fisheries income but conflict over ownership has disrupted management and prevented their full potential being realized (see photograph 5).

Both settlements suffer the constraints to livelihoods typical of the char regions (Box 2.3).

The Practical Action research team had assumed that the social and institutional environment of the recently settled village of Nadagari would prove a more receptive setting for consensus building and participatory planning through PAPD. The community would be more homogeneous in terms of livelihood activities (a dependency on crop-based agriculture), widening the opportunity for agreement.

Photo 5   Fishing at Nandina waterbody

Box 2.3   Displacement, conflict and environmental shock in the chars

One 35-year old male resident of Nadagari (Minal) reported being displaced nineteen times since childhood during which time he has lived with friends and family within a seven to fifteen kilometre range of the village. This migrant lifestyle is typical of those that settle new chars and have no ability to secure land.

Settlement of Nadagari took the form of a land grab and the effects of this have been long-lasting. Individual households are still struggling to secure legally or locally recognized property rights and violent conflict has resulted. Disputes are exacerbated by the intrusion of party politics at this level and perceived political bias or corruption. The Nadagari settlers were displaced from several adjacent villages after the erosion of the river bank and the village remains socially isolated from its 'parent' settlements. The mix of households from separate communities with distinct social traditions and relations has created natural 'fault lines' for conflict to emerge.

By contrast, the growth of Nandina since the arrival of the first settlers has almost entirely been endogenous and land disputes are much less common.

Natural resource conflicts in the char villages centre on access to, and the control of, government owned khasland and associated waterbodies. Both these land and water resources are de jure open access but are normally commandeered by the most influential, making asset accumulation by the poor almost impossible. Fisheries are frequently controlled by absentee lessees acting as exploitative *jotedars* (middlemen) situated between government institutions and the poor.

All char settlements must adopt coping strategies for the disruptive annual flood. The last major flood occurred in 1998 but there were serious floods in the area during 2004 that caused hunger, disease and the displacement of many people.

In contrast, it was thought that the relative diversity of interests and livelihoods at established Nandina might prove an obstacle to planning and that the demand for livelihoods development might be less pressing. The team had assumed that the more mature settlement at Nandina was more socially complex and that planning would be stifled by long-lasting and ingrained land and water disputes.

As expected, the key constraints to consensus and community-level planning were social/institutional ones. However, Practical Action's hypothesis that the recently settled village may offer greater opportunities for PAPD and consensual planning was later proved false: recently settled char communities are often fractured and comprised of relatively disparate family groups or *gusthi* (see *Local influencers and the evolution of new institutions*). This has consequences for the degree of cohesion, unity and support provided through social capital and the likelihood of balanced negotiation and planning.

The preparatory phase involved a scoping study to assess livelihoods constraints and the nature of conflict and cooperation in the two charland villages. Informal discussions with the poor and other stakeholders were used to break the ice and to increase the team's awareness of key local issues and relationships. The strategy was to spend sufficient time to identify opportunities for building consensus and to ensure that different stakeholder groups were equally mobilized and prepared for the process. Preparatory phase activities may need to include the mobilization of interest groups, raising the capacity of certain groups, and ensuring good channels of communication between potential PAPD participants and the stakeholder group they may be representing. The core group formation activity pursued by Practical Action was participatory technology development (PTD).

Participatory Technology Development (PTD)

The PTD process implemented by Practical Action Bangladesh encourages technical choices by farmers and facilitates farmer innovations by helping to source technical and expert support through local representatives known as rural community extensionists (RCEs). Villagers select a handful of farmers to receive extra training from Practical Action in veterinary and cropping issues. The RCEs are given advice and additional support from technical service providers including government agriculture and livestock officers. The formation of PTD groups with a wide range of producers and stakeholders (including small holders, full-time fishers and other landless and women) helps create a platform for discussion of interrelated problems for char dwellers such as sources of seed and credit, market opportunities, linkage and relationships with service delivery organizations and personnel. The PTD initiatives were designed to enhance group dynamics and unity, interaction, bargaining power and interaction through discussion and planning in the villages (photograph 6).

PTD represented an opportunity to instil a planning mindset and to raise the confidence of the poor and the most marginalized.

Photo 6   Goat vaccination with a rural community extensionist

Example 1: PTD to enhance maize and chilli production

Agricultural activity is the main livelihood option for char dwellers. Chilli is a major cash crop of the villagers of Nadagari but they were facing many constraints, resulting in low yields. Earlier scoping studies had revealed that the main cash crop, chilli, was badly affected by soil borne and seed borne diseases each year and the char people had prioritized the need to address this loss in production and to try maize as a complementary crop (photograph 7).

Practical Action Bangladesh came forward jointly with a government body, the Regional Agriculture Research Station (RARS), to provide technical support and inputs to the farmers. Some maize seed was provided by RARS and farmers purchased extra seed with cash support from a partner NGO, Unnayan Sangha.

The main objective was to reduce the risk and vulnerability of char dwellers in chilli farming by introducing maize as an alternative or supplementary crop. Some farmers mono-cropped maize, some used maize as a border/dyke crop with chilli and other farmers used maize as an intercrop with chilli.

The average maize production rate was 2.4 tonnes per acre in all three cases. This was a low yield in comparison to standard production rates in other regions of Bangladesh but low input costs meant that the cost–benefit ratio was seen as acceptable from these poor soils. In short, maize production appeared viable and was locally valued.

Maize farmers moved from an individual farmer approach to a collective approach, planning together to attract the support and advice of technical service providers for the char villages (photograph 8). Through this maize initiative, farmers were brought into regular contact and started discussing

Photo 7   Chilli sales at Nadagari

Photo 8   Women processing the new maize crop

Table 2.1   The trend in winter vegetable cultivation in the two char villages

Location	% of households producing winter vegetables			
	Pre 2002	2002	2003	2004
Char Nadagari	10%	24%	52%	80%
Char Nandina	<50%	54%	63%	90%

broader local issues such as the limits to local infrastructure and how new community planning structures might gain greater influence and harness outside support.

Example 2: PTD to help establish winter vegetable cropping

Charland farmers are generally wary of attempting mixed vegetable production because of the extreme risk of flood damage. Over the period 2002 to 2004 around 75 per cent of households in the two char villages received training in soil and crop management for improved winter vegetable production. In 2004 there were three floods in one season and heavy rainfall hampered vegetable production but the training ensured that vulnerability was reduced and production could continue. The producers favoured quick growing and leafy vegetable varieties like radish, red amaranths, white amaranths, spinach and coriander, planted with no tillage in silt-laden land after the flood.

Because of the short culture period after the flood, villagers raised their seedlings early and in protected high seedbeds within the homestead or on raised areas within the villages. Farmers made their own choice of vegetable production and shared experiences on bottle gourd, *brinjal* (aubergine/egg plant), radish and cauliflower production and pit cultivation. The number of vegetable producers increased in this period due to the new skills of the villagers and the high market price of these crops (Table 2.1).

This PTD initiative identified suitable vegetable production strategies with local farmers. The high market value, combined with risk management intended to prolong the growing period, ensured that winter cropping became attractive and widely supported (photograph 9). Just as significantly, this PTD established new relationships between local farmers and service providers.

In summary, simple confidence-building activities and technical cooperation between external service

Photo 9   Harvest of the winter vegetables

providers and rural community extensionists were intended to make modest but early breakthroughs and to underline the value of collective planning. Practical Action's strategy was to move from these smaller, low-risk interventions, to larger, cross-cutting and mutually beneficial plans and actions.

The aim was to apply the PAPD principles in a less bounded manner, using the various tools as pressing issues emerged and as or when the community expressed a need for facilitation or guidance.

It was important to develop and understand the capacity of the villages to participate in cross-cutting planning as early as possible and visual evidence of the benefits of simple consensus planning were required by the communities. Both villages proposed the construction of their own community houses as a neutral place to hold meetings, discuss issues and to provide shelter during the flood. The process of negotiation that went into these plans was illuminating for both the facilitating team and the community (see Box 2.4).

Navigating the local social and institutional landscape – experience from the char villages

All facilitated development initiatives have a social and informal institutional component. In Bangladesh, many past technical projects have inadvertently introduced conflicts or polarized the positions of different livelihoods groups. Often those most able to benefit (the entrepreneurial, the politically influential, those able to afford investments of time and money) can exploit new

---

Box 2.4   Planning for the new community houses

Early in the process of community planning, the goal was to achieve a unifying and useful outcome as evidence of the benefits of local negotiation and collaboration. Problem census revealed a need for a neutral meeting space in both villages and Practical Action offered to supply building materials once plans had been drawn up and siting agreed by the two communities.

In Nadagari the construction of the community house was unanimously approved by villagers in September 2003. The potential influence and social kudos to be gained through the donation of land for public use meant that landowners competed to provide the land for construction of the community house. The contest was initially between two landowners and when, after two months and five meetings, their differences could not be resolved, a third person was nominated. The house was eventually located at the end of his homestead area, to the south of the village, on an area previously used as a cow pen. The contesting landowners withdrew on condition that the land would be registered with the Land Office in the name of the newly formed village committee. However, the third landowner, who became responsible for 'maintaining the house', still clearly anticipated personal benefits – for example he took it on himself to lend out the solar panel provided by Practical Action (to light the house and raise revenue by charging batteries) for social/ceremonial functions. Subsequently the two unsuccessful landowners called on their *gusthi* clan to boycott the use of the community house.

Similar problems were avoided in Nandina by locating their community house on an already communal plot of land in the village bazaar. A shopkeeper was allowed to power a light in his shop in return for watching over the house.

opportunities while the most vulnerable find themselves excluded and disadvantaged. Development projects introduce a kind of social and institutional flux as different groups realign their positions, form new relationships and allegiances or exploit their influence to support or block change. This is particularly the case where interventions provide sudden gains through subsidized inputs or subsidized rights of access (Lewins, 2004).

Practical Action's experience working with the char communities at Nandina and Nadadgari was rather different because it was engagement with a planning process itself, rather than the physical end point (a community building or boat etc.), that was the goal. The research team had to track and understand the community's stance towards local planning and the significance of the various obstructions to progress. In doing this, the team were better able to understand the significance of consensus and any breakthroughs when they did occur.

In this case, the open and public use of PAPD was seen by some as a direct challenge to existing social factions (*gusthi*). However, these same groups recognized the potential for PAPD to release political and financial support for local initiatives. They found that they had to keep engaged and prevent themselves becoming isolated and irrelevant.

Village institutions

The consensus building theory highlights the importance of understanding public 'positions' and private 'interests'. The intention in the char villages was to work with these background interests in mind and to accommodate them whenever possible. Practical Action conducted a review of social institutions in the two villages and of their significance to community planning with PAPD. Focus group participants were asked to rank their village institutions within the broad definition given above. In both villages the mosque was cited as most important, people explaining 'we are Muslims!' i.e. spiritual life was placed above secular. Participants were then asked to consider the importance of the secular institutions alone. In Nandina, the community groups associated with Practical Action (especially the waterbody management committee – see later) and the *masjid* (mosque) committee were jointly assigned greatest importance. The Gram Sharkar tier of local government was deemed 'less effective'.[18]

Villagers were asked about the significance of *gusthi* kinship groups in their communities and the larger mixed groups of *gusthi* known as *bonghso*. They described these as inherited social characteristics where *gusthis* form branches of the larger *bongshos*. They added: 'there is free intermarriage between *gusthi* clans – unlike Hindu castes'. The system is patrilineal and membership designated by a shared surname. However, the frequent recurrence of common surnames indicates that this alone is insufficient to define a *gusthi*. In the past some *gusthi* were associated with specific occupations, though this is less common today. Traditionally one, occasionally two, influential households led *gusthis*, and this is still often the case in the two char villages.

There are three key *gusthis* in Nandina. All the Sharkars and most of the Mondals and Mullahs are related to the original settlers of the village about 80 years ago. In recent times, more male Mondals from Madargonj and Bogra have married back into the village owing to land pressure elsewhere.[19] Most Sharkars are located in the south of Nandina village, and Mondals to the north.

The pattern of settlement in Nadagari has resulted in greater mixing of different *gusthi* groups but the Mondals are the dominant group.

The discussion with villagers suggested that although *gusthi* allegiances remain important in terms of social interaction and hierarchy, land pressure and the encroachment of party political and 'democratic' institutions in village life have to an extent reduced their influence.

There are several important mosque-related institutions in the village that have influence over local decision-making and everyday life. The *jama't masjid* (Friday mosque) hosts five daily services, including the main weekly and best-attended prayers on a Friday. More numerous and smaller general mosques cater mainly for daily prayers. A *jama't* mosque will typically serve one or more villages whereas individual *paras* (neighbourhoods) within a village may each have their own 'general' mosque. There is one *jama't* mosque in Nandina and one *jama't* and one general mosque in Nadagari. The Nandina mosque is the largest and finest building in the village, while both Nadagari mosques are of more modest construction.

Each mosque has a board of trustees known as the *masjid* committee, comprising influential community members. The committee is primarily responsible for the upkeep and management of the mosque and the recruitment of an imam. The committee also undertakes other important social functions; most significantly, informal dispute mediation and conciliation through *salish*. This remains the main mechanism for dealing with low level, civil disputes. Only when *salish* fails do aggrieved parties resort to law courts which involve greater expense, potential escalation and the entrenchment of conflicts. Most villagers appear to have greater confidence in the *salish* process. *Salish* sessions usually take place after Friday prayers at the *jama't masjid*. An example of a *salish* resolution is presented in Box 2.5.

Traditionally, considerable influence and status is accrued to the family who donate land for construction of a mosque and such households tend to be well represented on local committees and institutions. In Nadagari, for instance, a rich man who donated land for the *jama't* mosque went on to hold an executive position on the PAPD committee. Similarly, residents of Nandina wished to include an influential head of the *masjid* committee from a neighbouring village in their PAPD process.

Box 2.5   *Salish* in Nadagari

A shallow-tube-well diesel pump was stolen from Giash and others in the village approached the influential *mathbor* to resolve the problem. When the first *salish* failed, some encouraged Giash to file a court case but a second *salish*, facilitated by a well-respected ex-UP member, successfully resolved the problem and avoided legal action. About five to ten of the local villages in the area now invite this man to help resolve the more complex *salish* cases. In this instance, the thief agreed to return the remains of the pump he had stripped for spare parts, plus 5,000 Tk. in compensation.

In both villages, the members of different *masjid* committees liaise to solve trans-boundary disputes between neighbouring *paras* or communities and these functions are valued by the vulnerable. The Practical Action team were encouraged by the way in which these established village institutions and social mechanisms were being utilized by local people to help the PAPD process succeed. The legitimacy of *salish* and the mosque, for instance, meant that both villages were actively seeking to integrate aspects of the *masjid* committee (its membership and their roles) with the PAPD committee. This link was considered to add gravitas to the planning process and aid the resolution of local disputes and problems.

The range of local institutions has consequences for community planning in any setting but here the social history of the sites and the rigid delineation of family groups proved more significant to the process than expected. Some of the planning problems encountered at the villages related to the delineation of the PAPD process. In Nadagari, Practical Action chose to test the PAPD approach with a workable subset of approximately 200 of the 2,000 households of 'Greater' Nadagari. In doing this, the project excluded some neighbouring family, friends and *gusthi* members of the participants.[20] No similar problems were encountered in Nandina, where the entire community of around 600 households was incorporated in the project area.

The Practical Action team now had a greater understanding of the local social and institutional features of the two villages. This early planning experience suggested that of the two villages, only Nandina was well placed to move to the next stage and to sustain a PAPD process around a 'high risk' issue. No opportunity for an equivalent PAPD initiative was identified in Nadagari during the period of the project. However, the difficulty of identifying a mutually acceptable plan with widespread support in this setting was instructive to the Practical Action team and is discussed below. The next section discusses in detail the evolution of a major community action plan through PAPD over a period of nearly two years in Nandina village.

PAPD phase: Community management of the waterbody in Nandina

The sequence of discussion, fact-finding, group formation and implementation that evolved between 2003 and 2005 was a reflection of the quality of facilitation and the enthusiasm of the community. Practical Action ensured that the principles of PAPD were retained and understood but the political complexity of the issues uncovered meant that the community had to negotiate problems over an extended period of time. Many of the problem areas were discussed and resolved 'offstage' rather than in public. *Gusthi* groups would discuss the plans in the evening and away from the facilitators before presenting their opinions and suggestions back to the wider community. Sometimes these positions caused setbacks to the process but often they represented proactive modifications to strategy, developed by the poor and later accepted by the majority. It seems that this greater flexibility added legitimacy through local ownership of the process.

The process was not a linear one, with several issues being discussed simultaneously. The following summarizes the key stages in the planning process at Nandina and provides the approximate period of time required to accomplish the task. A bad flood meant that planning-related issues were put on hold by Practical Action and the community between October 2003 and January 2004.

Familiarity and issue-identification (January–March 2003)

The prospect of creating a community-managed fishery from the permanent waterbody in Nandina had been the subject of local speculation since Practical Action started work on the consensus-building project in 2003. While smaller, technical initiatives (such as pit composting, animal husbandry and veterinary support) were taking place, both the community and Practical Action began to discuss the opportunities provided by the waterbody. Local residents viewed the waterbody as an under-utilized resource and Practical Action saw it as a potential flagship for promoting collective planning and management in the future.

Information gathering and sharing (April–June 2003)

The community recognized that the key constraint to developing the waterbody for public use related to ownership. Practical Action facilitated a process by which community volunteers investigated the legal status of the waterbody and approached secondary stakeholders such as the Upazila Fisheries Officer and the Land Office for relevant information.

The villagers were aware that travelling fishers would use the waterbody periodically, claiming permission had been granted from an owner outside Nandina. The main issue for the villagers was whether this was a state-registered *jalmohal* where a lease was payable to government, or an informal arrangement where a 'private' waterbody had been illegitimately commandeered by an entrepreneur.

After several weeks' discussion with the Land Office and the Upazila administration it transpired that the waterbody was not, in fact, registered as a *jalmohal* by the government (see Box 2.6). Maps and documentation had been obtained from the Land Office and the status of the waterbody was reported back to the community at an open meeting. The implications for community planning were discussed immediately – it was possible that a detailed plan for community management might see access granted to the villagers of Nandina.

Supportive stakeholders included the State Minister of Planning and Finance (also the local MP) and the District and Upazila Fisheries Officers. The Minister provided a key role in directing the police department of Sarishabari Upazila to protect the village from intimidation by outsiders and to switch their allegiance from the illegal occupier of the waterbody. Even with this support, though, the community recognized the need for an organized and collective management plan to gain official approval. A major concern at this stage was the risk of the waterbody becoming registered as a *jalmohal* because local people would not be able to compete with richer individuals in the open auction process of leasing.

Box 2.6   Investigating the legal status of the Nandina waterbody

Background: In Bangladesh all recorded inland fisheries are defined as *jalmahals* (water estates) and are administered by the Ministry of Land. Since 1950 there have been numerous policy changes that have attempted to modify the way in which access to the fisheries is managed and who ultimately benefits. In 1995, the Government of Bangladesh declared that all open waterbodies (including rivers, canals and floodwater) would be exempt from the leasing system in order to allow access by the poor.

A delegation of Nandina community volunteers revealed illegitimate management of the village waterbody. Several individuals were exploiting confusion over the status of the waterbody and a lack of awareness of access rights by the poor.

During high flood, the Nandina waterbody is connected with another *jalmohal* – Roha Kolishakori Jalkor – defined as a closed waterbody and leased by a dubious cooperative residing outside the village. These owners have been illegally prosecuting the Nandina waterbody during the flood season and collecting fees from village fishers with the support of their local *mastaan* (thugs).

The Nandina volunteers found that these individuals had the support of key administrative institutions at district level and that many open waterbodies in the area were still routinely registered as 'closed' in order to retain revenue collections. The Department of Fisheries, the Land Department and several party political individuals were active in challenging this anomaly, however, and Practical Action and the village volunteers were successful in gaining sufficient political backing for a community management plan.

To date, Roha Kolishakori Jalkor continues to be leased by the same group but their access to village waters has been successfully blocked by the community. The PAPD stocking initiative (see later) continues unchallenged in the village.

The process of information gathering and public debate has made secondary stakeholders at UP, Upazila and district level aware of Nandina's community initiative and of the common misinterpretation of the leasing system, more generally. It has also introduced villagers to the workings of those formal institutions that are supposed to represent their interests and opened up channels for continued dialogue. In this respect, the PAPD process has helped challenge the deliberately opaque access arrangements that prevent the poor from using their land and water entitlements.

There was also concern that the 'outsiders' currently exploiting the waterbody would remain better placed to influence the corrupt leasing system.

Group formation (February 2004)

Practical Action noted that the community aligned themselves into about seven basic interest groups on the basis of their stake in the waterbody: (1) richer, large landowners adjacent to the waterbody; (2) richer landowners with less land; (3) poor – with or without land; (4) poorer – no land/homestead only; (5) fishers; (6) women; and (7) waterbody leaseholders (four village fishers sub-contracting access from the external entrepreneur). These groups were not mutually exclusive, however, so that women might air their opinions during discussions held by the landless, for instance.

Each group was encouraged to hold their own informal meetings to discuss the obstacles to community management of the waterbody and potential solutions. The Practical Action team were encouraged to note that these issues were communicated informally to households within and between groups. The range of issues encapsulated both technical constraints and social or institutional obstacles (see Table 2.2).

A key feature of this stage was the way in which issues were uncovered and resolved by the groups without the need for formal facilitation and planning meetings – what the Practical Action team described as 'offstage' negotiation. Here we come to a key breakthrough in the Nandina consensus-building process. The opposition of the external waterbody leaseholder was overcome by winning over his supporters within the village. The role of *gusthi* factions was crucial in this process. The Practical Action staff were not party to any of these discussions and negotiations, but they came to understand that the external leaseholder had relatives in the village who were arguing his case. However, these relatives were inter-married with influential supporters of the village waterbody management plan. Three or four months of intensive discussions were required within the leaseholder's *gusthi* group before that group agreed to come forward and participate in the new village scheme. The external leaseholder became progressively isolated within the village and after some short-lived attempts at

Table 2.2 Concerns over community management of the Nandina waterbody

Interest group	Community waterbody concern/issue
Rich landowners adjacent to waterbody	Discussions centred on shares of benefits (landowners assumed a share on basis of land area) and improved access to fish seed. Practical Action was concerned that some in this group – with vested interest in current informal leasing system – could block change.
Poor – no land adjacent to site	This group was wary of richer interests and strategies – minimizing total costs might reduce the influence of the rich, they suggested. There are serious technical constraints to stocking including weed control.
Poor – landless	Proposed an equal share of benefits and the right to donate labour rather than capital. The group were concerned that any management committee would be transparent and believed the rich could not manage alone. Fingerling costs seen as a major constraint.
Full-time fishers	Felt they must have significant input due to greater fishery knowledge but worried that their status would reduce their input. May have required some compensation from controls on fishing. Recognized the need for village unity to deter outside interference. Weed control and fingerling costs seen as major technical constraints.
Women	Women were motivated by the prospect of increased fish consumption and felt they could contribute to the processing (drying) stage. A full role may boost technical skills for their own pond cultivation but women were worried their input would be blocked by the wider community (women had not had a labour role such as this before).

intimidation, gave up his campaign. By this stage the planning process had reached a level of public legitimacy that meant that police refused to investigate the leaseholder's false allegations of corruption against the community leaders (photograph 10).

The outcome of this intra-*gusthi* bargaining and the drop in threats and intimidation that resulted was marked. The general unity brought about by the PAPD process was deemed to have reduced the significance of political affiliations and the villagers had achieved a space free from the penetration of macro-politics and violence. Although the majority of villagers were traditionally aligned with the ruling party, one waterbody committee member stated that if necessary they would now all vote together strategically!

As the Practical Action field staff went about their work during these months, they came across examples of the rising confidence and influence of poorer community members in village affairs and the growing sense of democratic village mobilization. The following examples are taken from the team member diaries, kept to record the process and to highlight social and institutional progress.

One woman from the poorest section of the community, Morion, and two others approached me in the village market and asked me about progress with the waterbody plan. They said that they were still not formally involved in the discussions and wanted to join – 'if we can join then we will contribute to the operation of the stocking scheme'. The possibility of joining then spread through the women's credit and savings group, the whole group was inspired. This was discussed with the

Photo 10   Gusthi meeting on the waterbody issue after Friday prayers

community leader and the women joined the PAPD process formally. This change demonstrated to everyone that the participation of women as a separate interest group was not something artificially imposed by Practical Action.

(Salma Begum, Research Associate, Practical Action)

At one plenary session, participants decided that they needed an extra day of discussion. An evening meeting was convened to share the plenary session progress, informing everyone of the proposed contribution of 300–500 Tk. This was agreed at 300 Tk and the 26 member Executive Committee was formed. In the Planning Meeting that ensued, there was intense bargaining over the profile of the committee with respect to involvement by the poorer groups – 'Why are all our names at the bottom of the list?' The result was that the list was mixed up with one of the poorest participants now made Vice President and agreement that the poor should be specially represented in the handling of money. One influential person was relegated to a general member.

(Asraf Uddin, Research Associate, Practical Action)

In May I visited the tea shop and listened in to a discussion. Complaints against Practical Action were coming left, right and centre, the previous leaseholder for the waterbody was there, stirring things up. An old man told a story about how a village leader's son graduated first class, but how his father had convinced the son to be a teacher in the village. It was a simple story about leadership and development and showed acute appreciation that the logic of the PAPD process was to promote greater village self-reliance. It was an example of how older people bring understanding of the process to the community.

(Kamal Hossain, Research Associate, Practical Action)

First plenary (May 2004)

Nearly three months later, Practical Action facilitated a public plenary for joint feedback between the interest groups. Each group presented its main concerns and priorities as a poster and the entire group then ranked these issues in order of importance. Potential solutions were negotiated for each of the issues in turn (see Table 2.3).

Committee formation (May–June 2004)

Practical Action facilitated the formation of a subgroup which was to be responsible for the management of public meetings and to keep all groups informed of developments – the waterbody management committee – but the structure of this committee and its function was largely the product of community discussion. Prior to the second public plenary, group representatives approached Practical Action with a draft committee outline. The executive committee was to comprise no more than 30 individuals and would work to ensure the fair and transparent management of a share system, open to 250 to 300 households in the village, and with each household contributing about 500 Tk. for an equal share of the harvest. As highlighted by the team's diary notes above, the first proposed structure of this committee was controversial with women and landless

Table 2.3   Early community resolutions on waterbody management

Issue and rank	Community resolution/commitment
1. Sustaining unity	Unity has discouraged illegal access to date – it can also help to ensure sustainable management in future
2. An acceptable allocation system	Some of the richer stakeholders committed to an equal share system
3. A respected committee	All interest groups agreed to contribute representatives to a future management committee
4. Access to local fingerlings	The village will attempt to raise its own fingerlings
5. Financial investment	Investments in the scheme should relate to ability to pay
6. Transparent accounting	Regular updates on expenditure and income to be posted in community building
7. Control of aquatic weeds	Grass carp can be introduced to control the weed
8. External support	The committee must stay engaged with the Fisheries officials and government stakeholders for continued support
9. Benefits to poor and women	Special arrangement will be made for fishers and female-headed households

stakeholders under-represented and unwilling to provide their full support to it. Practical Action found it necessary to facilitate a re-think of committee structure – encouraging the election of several 'poor' individuals to the committee.

In parallel with the waterbody plan, Practical Action was facilitating other local initiatives including livelihoods diversification and training. The community had prioritized the construction of a community building as a neutral space for the planning of these activities and as a flood shelter. These activities had worked to gradually build the planning capacity of the community and its familiarity with a range of informal community committees.

Second plenary (May 2004)

By this stage, the interest groups had discussed the outcomes of the first plenary and the function of the waterbody management committee. However, a second plenary was necessary to ensure all Nandina residents were made aware of progress and could contribute to the waterbody action plan. In this regard, the plenary represented a knowledge-sharing process between poor primary stakeholders rather than an effort to secure the support of political and technical secondary stakeholders. It was an opportunity to report back the progress made on securing the backing from these service providers and political stakeholders.

The meeting focussed on overcoming the obstacles and of ways to pre-empt management problems before they occur. The result was a provisional community action plan (CAP) detailing the social, technical, financial and institutional requirements for success (see Table 2.4).

Table 2.4 Specific management requirements identified during the second public plenary

	Management requirements
Social	• Special provision will be provided to women and female-headed households (5% of profits to be allocated to the poorest)
	• Each household will have the opportunity to take part
	• Villagers will share guarding duties
	• A policy for enrolment of others must be decided in future
Technical	• Fish sanctuaries will be used to boost local fish (*deshi mach*) species
	• Nets and bamboo enclosures to protect fish stock
	• An additional flood-protected pond to be leased for fish seed production
Financial	• 300–500 Tk. membership is affordable to most and sufficient for first year
	• A monthly wage will be provided to the poorest guards
	• Harvesting time according to market price – local traders to will be used
	• Committee to reinvest a share of profits (approx. 20%) and redistribute the rest equally to participating households
	• A provisional budget of 150,000 Tk. will cover first year costs
Institutional	• The committee will operate a joint account with transactions requiring unanimous decision
	• Expenditure and profits to be posted in community building
	• Banks, NGOs, Practical Action and the Department of Fisheries to be lobbied for extra support for fencing and stocking
	• A professional fish seed merchant to be enlisted from outside the area

Implementation (June 2004)

In 2004, approximately 200 households became ordinary members of the WBMC, all of whom donated 300 Tk. towards stocking, netting and harvesting of the waterbody. Shares were limited to one per village household but the popularity and anticipated potential of the plan resulted in a great many more households joining until about 400 households (most of the village) were involved (photograph 11).

A year later, and in the light of the first full cycle of fish production, the community made several changes to the management approach. Of the 31 member WBMC, 14 'poor' and 4 women members were retained but the Chairman had been unable to provide sufficient time and was replaced by mutual consent. Four villagers were expelled from the scheme for cheating the harvesting and selling process and, according to the Practical Action team, it was poor members who were active in removing these individuals.

The committee continues to meet about twice a week during the peak fish culture season and as and when waterbody issues arise during the off-season.

Although the first harvest generated a profit, the community made several modifications to intensify production. Firstly, the WBMC began actively seeking credit inputs from a local partner NGO to Practical Action – Rural Development and Social Mobilization (RDSM). In 1995, RDSM provided a 40,000 Tk. loan and effectively doubled the investment available to operation costs. Two full-time guards were employed to protect the waterbody and these were supported by 10 groups of volunteers that alternated their watches in the evenings.

Several technical changes were made. It was agreed that the full length of the growing season should be better exploited and that fingerlings should be introduced as soon as possible after the flood water had dispersed. The

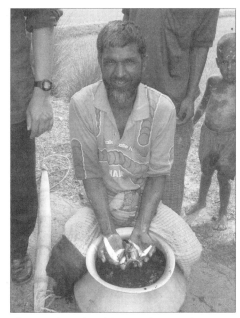

Photo 11   A local fry vendor supplying fish for stocking

fingerling size would also be increased to maximize the harvest weight and sale price.

In all, these changes represent encouraging social (community cooperation, self-policing etc.) and institutional (new links with RDSM and sustained modes of management) developments. The process since the facilitated PAPD has been self-organizing and there are indications that the broad management and planning approaches will continue to operate in Nandina.

Local influencers and the evolution of new institutions

This section offers a comparative analysis of the project experience in the two sites, highlighting lessons learned on the nature of prevailing socio–cultural realities in isolated and attached chars.

Nadagari

Many of the decision-making difficulties encountered in Nadagari, that prevented 'high-risk' PAPD activities, relate to social divisions which can be traced back to the geographical origins of the villagers. While most households originate from the original mainland Nadagari village and belong to the Mondal *gusthi*, over 10 per cent came from the neighbouring village of Shuknagary. Friction between these two groups is aggravated by the greater political influence of Shuknagary (the MP comes from the village) and there is a certain level of mistrust and suspicion between the *gusthi*.

The Practical Action team was able to identify three key influencing groups based on their allegiance: (1) the Nadagari Mondals; (2) the Shuknagary and other 'outsider' stakeholders; and (3) local individuals less clearly aligned to *gusthi*.

Practical Action found that most of the negative politicking that occurred around the PAPD process was between these first two groups and that this was itself rooted in the continuing land struggle. The third, more passive, group of influencers was said to 'suffer' as a result.

One of the most significant activities facilitated by Practical Action in Nadagari was the construction of a community house but the planning process was very much moulded by these *gusthi* factions (Box 2.4). The social and political status enjoyed by the provision of such public spaces meant that influential landowners competed to provide the land for the building and disrupted the planning process. Similar problems were avoided in Nandina by locating the community building on an already communal plot in the village market.

The Practical Action team was well aware of the dynamics between and within the local factions, the motives of the various leaders and challengers, and their pro-poor credentials. During the course of this planning process several contentious issues were played out and eventually resolved – most of these concerning representation and leadership.

An initial planning committee was elected during a meeting attended by 'almost all' villagers. However, both Practical Action and some of the villagers felt that this original committee had been formed too quickly and was weak. The process was restarted and over the course of several community meetings the committee was reshaped until the successful completion of the community house eventually consolidated the role and function of the executive group (photograph 12).

Nandina

The negotiation process was slower in Nandina but the outcomes are perhaps more likely to be sustainable. Two years after Practical Action had introduced the PAPD planning process about 200 households had participated in group-related activities and PAPD planning for the village waterbody. As the community worked towards the stocking and management of the waterbody, the shape and function of the implementing committee became the key issue. A series of influential and well-respected ex-UP or businessmen were elected by the community to oversee an umbrella committee of 21 members including four secretaries with responsibilities for fisheries, livestock, agriculture and gender.[21] Practical Action was aware of the early power struggles and helped ensure pro-poor representation – encouraging the appointment of a female gender secretary and the inclusion of poor householders. The PAPD plan to stock the village waterbody required the WBMC as a sub-committee to coordinate the stocking, guarding and harvesting of fish. The WMBC members would meet informally every night at the tea stall next to the waterbody.

Before the formation of these committees, 'natural leaders' and influencers had convened periodic and issue-based meetings. The community planning ethic was not lost to the new committee structures and focus group discussion revealed the following:

Photo 12   Villagers celebrate the completion of the Nadagari community house

- Decision making had been more autocratic in the past, with 'influential leaders' taking the lead. With the formation of the committee, however, all participants recognized the need to establish roles for individuals and various factions such as the *gusthis*.
- Rather than one-off community-wide meetings, separate meetings were being held in each part of the village and surrounding area. Marginalized voices were more likely to be honoured and the Mondal *gusthi* became less dominant.
- Female representation had improved with four women formally represented on the PAPD committees. As one woman said: 'There has been a self-revolution! We have exposed weak points and strong points. There has been mental development and confidence building'.
- Before the PAPD committees were formed *salish* was the main means of resolving obstacles to PAPD. This has merely worked to maintain the status quo – elites demonstrated power by using *salish* as a political tool. Once the PAPD committees were operating with confidence, the coercion and violence associated with party political issues became of less concern: 'There is no party, now there is only the community committee party. If needed the whole village will support one party! The Gram Sharkar and committee members are now common, there are no conflicts. The Gram Sharkar may come or go with government, but the committee is stable'.

The successful negotiation of the waterbody plan was illustrative of progress in democratic decision making. As discussed, participants were originally representative of seven interest groups: (1) richer, large landowners adjacent to the waterbody; (2) richer landowners with less land; (3) better-off/with or without land; (4) poorer – no land/homestead only; (5) fishers; (6) women; and (7) waterbody leaseholders. During the final PAPD plenary session there was a major dispute over the allocation of future profits from the waterbody with the major landowner group demanding the greatest share. A meeting was held independently of Practical Action where the poorest group threatened to withdraw from the plan. The landowners ultimately agreed to an equal share of profits between the participants.

Practical Action posed various questions with respect to the key contributions of the PAPD planning process. The men felt that fish stocking, seed distribution and maize cultivation were the most practical outcomes. Women felt that the community house was a major development because they could now attend meetings and that the community now had shown increased patience, tolerance and self sacrifice: 'With your advice we climbed a tree, don't take away the ladder! When the boat starts sinking, if the boatman panics we all will die. We have just started learning!'

Summary

The review of social processes at the two villages suggests greater potential for beneficial and sustainable change at Nandina. Although a very similar PAPD process was working in Nadagari, there was some evidence that latent conflict was being inflamed. The apparent lack of social capital at Nadagari is probably consistent with other recently settled chars where newcomers originate from several towns and *gusthi* groups. This has obvious consequences for the broader applicability of the PAPD approach, both in the charlands and other settings.

Nandina, a longer settled and relatively affluent village, clearly has greater social cohesion than Nadagari. The ability to enact a major plan from the PAPD process was also instrumental in achieving broader acceptance and unity. There were no comparable cross-cutting and win–win opportunities in Nadagari.

In Nadagari, lack of secure title to recently settled land was one of the principle causes of division and this was compounded by social heterogeneity and project boundaries drawn up before the significance of the *gusthi* was fully appreciated. It should nevertheless be pointed out that beneath the surface of discord between *gusthi* groups, very important collective socio–economic gains and new linkages were achieved in Nadargari with respect to the improved production strategies in fisheries, livestock and crops developed with the community through PTD. Another positive indicator of change, according to the participants, is that at times of flood crisis, these *gusthi* differences disappear and improved social organization in the village is now evident in the efficient and equitable distribution of emergency food supplies to the poorest households

Nandina already had better political leverage with its two resident ex-UP members and good links to service-providing institutions. Practical Action hope that the successful negotiation of the waterbody plan will improve their bargaining position for accessing other waterbodies and khasland in the future.

Nandina's cohesion was also reflected in their successful cooperation with earlier development projects. Under a recent UNICEF water sanitation programme implemented by a local NGO, the community constructed an arsenic-free ground well with financial contributions from each household. In contrast, development initiatives in Nadagari have focussed on individual micro-credit and loans schemes that may have promoted a culture of dependency.

In both villages there was a desire to incorporate existing institutions such as *salish*. Here the informal process of committee formation allowed respected individuals, from structures such as the *masjid* committees and Gram Sharkar, to cross over to the PAPD process. Nandina's efforts to mobilize external support for their waterbody initiative benefited from the involvement of these important stakeholders.

Practical Action found that villagers tended to use existing resilient and influential institutions such as the *salish* as yardsticks when evaluating facilitated consensus building and planning. This has consequences for the promotion of PAPD elsewhere. Facilitators of rural development, in general, can do more to acknowledge those institutions that really do influence local outcomes. There is a need to generate more useable messages from institutional theory and to apply this to the reality on the ground. This means avoiding technical rhetoric and preconceived notions and indicators of institutional success (such as committee formation, the registration of CBOs or the establishment of constitutional rules etc.). Instead, facilitators should recognize existing 'ways of doing things' as informal institutions with pro-poor potential. Navigating this landscape with the poor means understanding, and working with, local notions of what comprises legitimate structures and processes for management and change.

The following chapter summarizes the use of the PAPD principles and stages in the char context and how the process was allowed to evolve over an extended period of time.

3

The char-modified PAPD approach

Practical Action found that the unique social and institutional features of the Bangladesh charlands necessitated an adaptive approach to consensual planning. Whilst it was possible to make progress on simple technical initiatives, the opportunities to challenge the deeper and underlying constraints to pro-poor change could only be addressed once a distinct level of trust had been built between the project team and the community. The facilitator is taken seriously once these 'difficult' issues are discussed in the open. The following chapter outlines in detail a modified approach to PAPD which works to help people navigate their own way through the technical, social and institutional constraints to development and change in the char context.

There are distinct parallels between some of Practical Action's approaches to rural development activities and facilitated, consensual planning such as PAPD. One of the functions of PAPD as it is normally applied in the Bangladesh floodplain is to identify early, attractive and cross-cutting examples of community planning in order to build social capital and mutual awareness between livelihoods groups. In this context, the intention is to gain momentum and a critical level of enthusiasm for other new pro-poor and sustainable practice or project activities.

In Bangladesh and elsewhere, Practical Action has been trying to facilitate change by building on modest technical improvements before tackling more intractable market and institutional issues relating to security, access rights and representation. In particular, 'low risk' technical interventions on fisheries, livestock and agriculture have been found to be a useful activity to 'break the ice' and prove the relevance of Practical Action as facilitator to local people and their immediate concerns. Local RCEs can support new activities by securing access to vaccinations and other inputs and can act as intermediaries between villagers and overstretched service providers. Normally, other related issues are aired and local people are encouraged to talk about wider-ranging constraints and opportunities to their livelihoods.

Practical Action's experience in the charlands suggests that the overall objective of local discussion and PAPD (consensus and planning) is best introduced gradually during a 'familiarity phase'. Technical support and facilitation with external service providers through engagement in livestock, fisheries or agriculture activities can build up the level of interaction, discussion and trust between the various stakeholders before moving on to broader cross-cutting planning through PAPD.

The stages of the char-modified approach

The char-modified planning process was extended considerably from the week-long workshop-based set of exercises (see Figure 1.4) to an eighteen-month process of interaction, discussion and facilitation. The following sequence is summarized in Figure 3.1.

Stage 1: Familiarity phase, issue identification

The initial stage of the char-modified PAPD approach introduces concepts of community planning, consensus and PAPD and attempts to uncover key livelihoods constraints in mixed group meetings. During this stage large or 'difficult' issues and problems are highlighted and potential solutions discussed informally. This process extends over a period of about nine days and the facilitating team assess the PAPD principles and tools in the light of the local and wider char context. A key modification at this stage relates to the disaggregation of the community and the joint selection of suitable representative groups for the planning stages. In the char context, interests and positions within social or kin groupings (*gusthi*) appear as significant as the livelihoods or resource user groups normally established with the facilitator during the workshop form of PAPD. The latter stages of the char-modified PAPD allow the interest groups to evolve independently and to represent concerns and suggestions informally.

In summary, this stage incorporates the PAPD tools of problem census and STEPS but draws back from formal planning sessions. Familiarity with the facilitating team grows and community enthusiasm increases with discussions and activities associated with simple day-to-day livelihoods constraints.

Stage 2: Information gathering and sharing, group formation, first plenary

Once problems and options have been aired, an information gathering process is established around a specific, unifying and cross-cutting prospective intervention. The researching and reporting responsibilities are delegated to community-identified representatives but the facilitating agency creates links with the relevant secondary stakeholders (in the case of the Bangladesh charlands, these groups will include Union- and Upazila-level government, the Land Office, and Union and Upazilla agriculture, livestock and fisheries agencies).

The wider community is updated of prospects and technical requirements for progress by the facilitator and the community researchers before a formal, open group meeting is held to discuss planning. The community develop several distinct groups in order to represent multiple interests and delegate responsibilities. These groups select their own representatives and allocate responsibilities for their members with minimal interference and facilitation. Each group's stance towards the planned action is discussed and potential problems/solutions identified before a plenary is held where the concerns and suggested alterations are presented and negotiated in public.

Stage 3: Committee formation, second plenary, implementation

The committee formation process is a gradual one and occurs in parallel with any technical agriculture, fisheries and livestock activities that have been planned with community groups additionally to PAPD negotiations. Committees, or what are termed locally as 'CBOs', are intended to be accessible and changing rather than fixed. By this stage, several participants will have experience of representing livelihood interest groups to Practical Action and other external stakeholders.[22]

Roles and responsibilities are confirmed and agreed in a public plenary. Key to this stage is the 'service negotiation' between the community and the secondary stakeholders invited to attend the meetings. The relevant sector-specific agencies are present and local political representatives are encouraged to publicly acknowledge and support declarations. The intention is to reach agreement on the timing and logistics of implementation. Finally, the action is initiated during a public ceremony.

The intervention is then modified and managed through interaction between the management committee and the wider community. The management committee is encouraged to meet on a regular basis and if the action plans are motivating and cross-cutting this process occurs with little or no facilitation.

Characteristics of the char-modified PAPD

The socio-economic, livelihoods and institutional setting of the charlands presents special challenges but consensus building and associated activities can tackle several development constraints simultaneously. Combining short- to medium-term technical activities can result in early changes to household income and reduce vulnerability, but the long-term effects that result from the experience of local planning and interaction with political and technical stakeholders are the key objective. These changes relate to social and political capital (vertical and institutional influence) and are intended to outlive the period of facilitation. It is hoped that the process of negotiation and collective action becomes normal i.e. is institutionalized. In the case of charland Bangladesh, PAPD appears capable of reinvigorating existing but under-utilized frameworks for service delivery and support.

Flexibility and careful facilitation is key to PAPD in the context of broad rural and social development that might transcend NRM issues. Char-modified PAPD uses the ability and willingness of local stakeholders to discuss and negotiate potential actions in an 'offstage' setting, independent of facilitated or formal workshop meetings.

It is absolutely essential to recognize the informal institutional environment that shapes legitimacy and the reality of decision making. In Bangladesh, for instance, it is often the traditional *salish* system of dispute resolution and mosque-related groupings (the *samaj*) that have the necessary legitimacy to arbitrate decisions. In the case of the charlands, the negotiation process may operate *within* independent *gusthi* groups rather than between different kinship groupings. Facilitating agencies must be able to work with these processes and interests and understand their local function and their potential contribution.

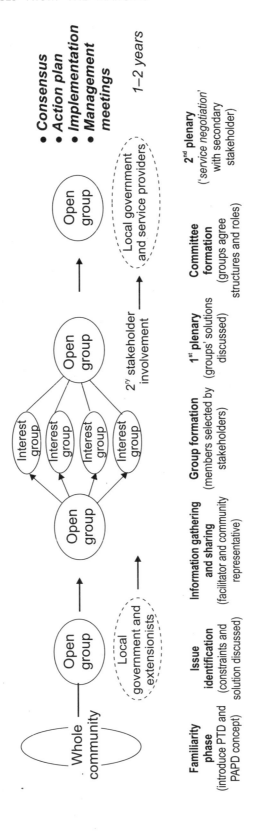

Figure 3.1 The char-modified PAPD approach for consensus building. The facilitator can apply PTD to maintain enthusiasm, build trust and linkages with secondary stakeholders. This PAPD is process based with regular formal/informal contact between community and facilitator over 12–24 months.

The charland communities that have worked with Practical Action have little previous experience with supportive NGOs. The local NGOs that have operated in the charlands are concerned with establishing profitable credit schemes but these are implemented according to national-level models, with little flexibility to adapt to local conditions. Charland poverty during the extended lean flood period is so acute that normal systems of weekly repayment break down, leading to acrimony between the NGOs and their defaulting borrowers. Given this setting, Practical Action recognized that any planning period needed to follow a lengthy familiarization phase whereby local people learned to trust facilitating personnel and their objectives.

Forcing the formation of groups is avoided. Rather, groups are allowed to evolve in relation to earlier technical support and problem-solving or emerging positions with respect to provisional community plans. As a result, group formation occurs relatively late in the process and, unlike the workshop-based PAPD, proceeding discussions are not based on livelihoods distinctions. There are several reasons for this. Firstly, interests (and constraints) in the charlands do not, in fact, break down to fisher versus farmer/landowner concerns. This relates to the relatively limited and agriculture-related livelihood activities and the nature of proposed activities and plans which tend not to be exclusively NRM related. Instead, planning discussions may centre on flood mitigation plans or the location and construction of a community building. Secondly, and perhaps most crucially, factionalism may relate as much to kinship differences (*gusthi*) as to occupational groupings. Each *gusthi* group might contain a range of livelihoods stakeholders and people of different socio-economic standing but obstacles to progress tend to relate to power struggles for influence between the *gusthi*.

When group formation is required to represent the concerns and objectives of different interests it may be lightly facilitated to ensure pro-poor representation. There is a trade-off here between allowing the planning process to evolve independently – increasing the sense of ownership and legitimacy – and ensuring that the process meets broad project/donor objectives. Ultimately, the way tools such as PAPD are applied relates to the experience and ability of the facilitator in question and the function that participation is intended to perform. PAPD will be most effective and meaningful when facilitated by agencies with the relevant community-level experience and as a component of projects or programmes that have far-reaching social and institutional development goals.

The key modifications summarized

1. Timing

PAPD is often applied as an introductory, ice-breaking activity to earn support for subsequent NRM project objectives and activities. In these settings, facilitators work intensively with stakeholder groups in a workshop setting and establish commitment on future action in five to eight days. However, the principles of PAPD, the need to breakdown mistrust between groups and then to channel this consensus into commitment with external support, lend themselves well to modification in different settings. The serious social and institutional constraints to planning in the chars required an extended period of relationship building with, and within, the community.

The planning phase can be extended when it occurs in parallel with simple PTD and support useful to, and popular with, the poor. The facilitating teams develop personal relationships and trust with a client group suspicious of outsiders and unused to interacting with NGOs and development projects.

The familiarization stage is intended to 'test the water' and to slowly develop a habit of interacting with service providers and political representatives. People become used to debating options and representing their own interests in a public setting. In the case of the PAPD at Nandina, these skills and the knowledge collected during early planning were transferred to the wider-reaching issue of community waterbody management.

From start to implementation, this form of PAPD may take between 12 and 24 months to achieve. The extended timeframe allows confidence building before tackling a major issue with powerful, external interest groups. The longer period is also a function of the setting (longer-term rural development projects/programmes) and the learning period required by the facilitators, themselves in the specialized char context.

Practical Action's experience suggests that momentum and confidence takes time to build in these isolated settings. Factions such as *gusthi* that can block or control change can be challenged by cross-cutting representation and by popular support for challenges to membership.

2. The role of formal institutions (service providers and political representatives)

As an extended process incorporating ongoing livelihoods enhancement and technical support, the involvement of secondary stakeholders in the char-modified PAPD is a greater priority than it may be in the NRM project context. Once roles and responsibilities have been established between the community and the facilitator, secondary stakeholders are more actively engaged in an ongoing process rather than at discrete points in time during a workshop setting. PAPD in the workshop format draws in secondary stakeholders during the public plenary sessions in order to provide gravitas to the occasion and place some pressure on local political stakeholders for continued support. The inclusion of these stakeholders does affect discussion quality, however, intimidating some and reasserting the power differentials between the poor and their representatives.

Secondary stakeholders appear more likely to provide the required support when the request is specific.[23] In this respect, the role of local government changes according to the phase of PAPD. During the pre-planning phase, local government bodies were relatively passive and any public pronouncements were routine and support seeking. However, once the planning stage proper had started and the scope and potential of the process became more obvious, the stance of these stakeholders became more supportive and facilitatory. During the information-gathering phase, local government may create a bridge between the facilitator and the community to the line department agencies and relevant administrative bodies.

Charlands are characterized by confusion and conflict surrounding property and access rights to both land and waterbodies. These issues may represent immediate obstacles to collective planning and require interaction with political and administrative bodies up to district level.[24]

In terms of technical service provision, char-modified PAPD forges relationships with under-utilized staff while community plans create a demand for inputs such as livestock vaccination, soil testing or crop demonstrations where previously there had been lacking knowledge of the options available. Local residents then form their own relationships with these staff, establishing mutual gains and potential sustainability.

Within this PAPD process, key local government individuals and institutions act as gatekeepers able to channel external funds or support from other political and service providing agencies.

3. The role of informal institutions (including elite and social factions)

Char-modified PAPD takes a pragmatic stance towards the 'problem' of entrenched power relations and strong local vested interests. For instance, it is often possible to use the political leverage of influential individuals with access to local government or service providers. These individuals can increase the perceived legitimacy of planning committees locally and elsewhere.

The social and demographic character of the chars vary but Practical Action experience suggests that more recently settled villages provide the greatest challenge to consensual planning.[25] However, Practical Action found that there was a local tendency to incorporate informal and existing institutions into PAPD. To some extent a reliance on the *salish*, mosque and the *samaj* indicates a preference by some poor to work through established power networks and to entrust decision making to their patrons. There are two main reasons why the status quo may tacitly be permitted to represent the poor on their behalf: (1) the political and social power these institutions provide reduce the transaction costs required to ensure implementation of decisions; and (2) it reduces the income-earning opportunities relinquished by the poor during their attendance at meetings.

It is widely acknowledged that elites and pre-existing power differentials can modify or destroy intended management structures and activities but there is also a growing recognition that it can be counterproductive to attempt to circumvent them completely – true consensus entails identifying win–win options than can satisfy the interests of all. However, the balance between facilitating an evolving local process and of over involvement (or interference) is a delicate one. Without careful scrutiny by the facilitating agency PAPD processes can be co-opted by the elite and it is important that staff have the capacity to conduct some form of social reconnaissance to identify potential supporters and catalysts for change.

While the quality and value of local planning may relate to geographic setting (biophysical characters, remoteness from markets, vulnerability to flooding, for instance), the strongest influencers appear social and institutional. Social and institutional mapping will highlight those site-specific characters that provide opportunities or obstacles to consensual planning. Many of these would relate to the informal institutional setting of the site in question such as personal allegiances within local government relating to *gusthi* or party politics, the function of the mosque committee, the level of respect for *salish* or the identity and interests of other elite.

4. The meaning of 'success'

The role and function of PAPD depends on setting and objective. In strongly facilitated projects with distinct NRM objectives, consensual community-level planning can be a useful mechanism to raise the level of awareness and support for more equitable or sustainable management and practice. In the case of the chars, social development and empowerment may be a more pressing requirement. There are several reasons for this. Firstly, these areas have little or no interaction with project-aligned agencies or NGOs. Work in this context cannot assume the future presence of these secondary stakeholders and must attempt to build lasting relationships with those institutions that *do* function and that *are* ubiquitous throughout rural Bangladesh – Union- and Upazila-level government bodies and staff, the *salish*, the mosque and patron–client relations. Once again, the overall aim here is to establish sustainable change and resilient institutions ('ways of doing things') not specifically institutions as structures like community-level committees.

A particularly pressing issue in the chars relates to security of access rights and tenure. Currently, allocation of private and khasland is controlled by a complex institutional melange representing the personal interests of privileged and political stakeholders and maintained by opaque process and deliberate obfuscation.

Practical Action has demonstrated that this institutional landscape can be navigated by local and poor stakeholders with the right facilitation and the right approach. The land and the waterbody required for these community initiatives was secured through a lengthy process of interaction and repeat visits to the Land Office and district level bureaucrats. The message here is that property rights can be negotiated for, and by, the poor and that the poor can be introduced to the formal and informal institutional workings of secondary stakeholders.

At the village level, PAPD has attempted to build cooperation between existing social factions. The *gusthi* at Nadagari represent an informal but resilient institution in its own right. Initially, differences between these groups represented a serious constraint to decision making and agreement but later on there were signs that younger and more pro-active individuals were challenging these local barriers.

Table 3.1   The characteristics of PAPD and char-modified PAPD

	PAPD	*Char-modified PAPD*
Setting		
– Biophysical and economic	Usually several floodplain villages with associated range of stakeholders and livelihoods interests.	To date, several char villages with restricted livelihoods options – limited production and market opportunities.
– Institutional	Facilitator often aligned with NRM project and/or other NGOs.	Facilitator has rural development remit. Minimal NGO and service provider presence.
Objective	Collective support of sustainable NRM arrangements through local planning and mutual learning.	Capacity to collectively engage with and influence formal and informal brokers – increased political capital.
Approach/timing	Workshop format with set activities conducted within and between livelihoods groups.	Some technical options discussed and adopted before residents move on to cross-cutting issues.
	Public declaration of support to plan by participants (subset of residents) and political representatives.	Informal groups evolve and hold independent meetings.
	Approx. eight day process with/without support for subsequent implementation of plans.	Facilitator supports an ongoing process of information gathering and lobbying over approx. 1–2 years.
Outcome/issues	Greater local understanding of NRM project objectives/ potential gains and planning experience.	Increased and sustained local political/institutional awareness, contact with service providers and experience with planning.
	Local support for new project resource management institutions (RMIs).	CBO(s) may evolve.
	Project-related planning then takes precedence.	Planning for general rural development options continues.

In summary, the purpose of PAPD in the charland context should be to form links with external institutions in order to release future support and collaboration. The livelihoods constraints in the chars largely relate to political and institutional isolation but Practical Action's experience suggests that this vacuum can be filled and that service providers can be encouraged to help solve problems associated with environmental setting and factors related to production.

These modifications are summarized in Table 3.1.

Synthesis

With skilled facilitation, char-modified PAPD has been able to help the vulnerable utilize local institutions and negotiate their access to land and water resources. In essence, the poor can be introduced to the formal and informal institutional workings of secondary stakeholders. The issue here is how sustainable this influence on social and institutional constraints really is.

The char-modified PAPD functions to forge relationships between the poor and the political stakeholders and service providers that are meant to represent them. Although Practical Action have in this case acted as a catalyst, injecting a base level of energy and incentive into the system, local people have been active in shaping the direction and form of dialogue that results locally and vertically with outside institutions. Community delegations to local government frequently took place without agency facilitation, for instance. In summary, char-modified PAPD can help release future support and collaboration from these stakeholders.

4
Discussion

Chapter 1 explored the application of consensus-building methodologies in development and how they have evolved in recent years. The analysis covered a range of experiences surrounding a central core theme; how consensus building has been applied to NRM and rural development in a variety of settings and for a range of purposes. This theme was developed in Chapters 2 and 3 by examining specific experiences from the Bangladesh charlands where the application of PAPD as a consensus-building approach has been tested.

As social, economic and environmental change intensifies conflict that impacts the poor, there is a strong case for transferring consensus-building principles from the context of isolated interventions and projects to planning for rural development more widely.

One step at a time

In 2001, the Bangladesh Practical Action team undertook an exploratory visit to one of the char villages. A large group of people gathered to discuss their needs and development priorities. The potential for consensus building in the chars was immediately apparent:

> *As general interest was high and people seemed open and clear, I decided to risk asking an elder how clear were the allocation of local land titles and deeds. Unfortunately the question was overheard by an onlooker who shouted: 'So, they have come to help me get back my land!' Within moments there was uproar. The man was manhandled away and while things calmed down almost as fast, this was a sharp reminder that addressing sensitive issues requires diplomacy. The elder's response was to ask for assistance on the issue, but to take one step at a time.*

(Barnaby Peacocke, Practical Action – field notes)

In the case of working with these char villages, then, there was a need for a tool that could engage local civil society and that could be quickly understood by staff and local partners including the poor. Ideally such a tool could be applied within a wide range of development settings. Ultimately, the relevance of PAPD can be attributed to its adaptability: the option, with good facilitation, to stretch the planning process where social and political features constrain change and are a risk to success.

These risks increase as the externalities from different livelihoods strategies impact and overlap with the interests of other groups, especially the powerful. In the charlands, low-risk planning prioritized support to production technologies or basic infrastructure where the interests and needs of all stakeholders could be accommodated. The consensus-building process can work quickly here, linking the poor to service providers, reinvigorating political stakeholders with new purpose and demonstrating mutual needs and the value of collective planning.

Higher-risk scenarios may be perceived locally as a direct challenge to the status quo. An initiative to help secure better access by poor fishers to a farmer-landowner's waterbody will interfere with fundamental local institutions ('ways of doing things'), for instance. Crude approaches can worsen social tensions by polarizing positions and losing credibility through early mistakes or failure. These scenarios require a combination of confidence building and time. Here, consensus building can work by focusing initially on low-risk entry points where benefits can be quickly experienced and observed. This opens up the potential of bringing different interests together to explore apparently more intractable issues. The principles and approach should stay the same, so that all stakeholders are aware of the purpose and process of planning, but it is given more time. Ultimately, participants should be left with positive experiences and a positive opinion of what has been achieved.

These low-risk and high-risk approaches are linked and can run in parallel because dialogue between producers and service providers (low-risk) builds the confidence of poor producers to negotiate with landowners and other political stakeholders (required for high-risk planning). Because formal government institutions have such limited presence in char villages, discussion and planning will operate along informal institutional lines like *gusthi* social factions. Although these social institutions may sometimes mute the voices of the poor, they can also operate to support and legitimize local planning. In the char villages of Jamalpur, Practical Action facilitated training on new cropping patterns, animal husbandry and fisheries management. The poor moved from these technical issues towards political issues with little need for encouragement.

With communities as vulnerable and politically isolated as those of the Bangladesh charlands, the confidence generated from early and tangible benefits to the poor seems a crucial precursor to action planning with the proper involvement of all stakeholders. In the case of Nadagari and Nandina villages, livelihoods support led to an immediate request by the poor for a democratic space: 'genuine debate and negotiation cannot take place on the wealthy man's porch'. The social kudos to be gained from donating the land for a community hall triggered an extended period of negotiation and favour-seeking by the wealthy. The poor were immediately immersed in discussion with individuals with real local influence.

The community had to operate within the existing system of land allocation that favours the powerful and relies on intimidation. The Practical Action team witnessed first hand the violence directed towards the legitimate but vulnerable claimants of emerging charlands. Despite this, fisheries-related plans proved useful in uncovering the rights of char residents and in exerting pressure on the institutions that were found to be failing the poor. A process of cautious and non-confrontational information gathering on the status of local common property resources like this mirrors the institutional mapping and participatory social reconnaissance used by some pursuing a 'rights-based' approach to rural development (see Bode, 2002). New knowledge sets the scene for creative problem-solving by the poor but because serious constraints, as well as opportunities, are made public, the process is an honest and empowering one.

The potential role of government structures

Many natural resource management projects in Bangladesh have placed great emphasis on the UP and continue to do so. Practical Action found that in the context of participatory planning, it seems that the UPs are most suited to consolidating the identity of potential beneficiaries/groups and in freeing-up resources from above. While they were found to be rather passive in the planning phase, they did add legitimacy and weight to plans at later stages. Once the time and costs of local planning had been invested by communities, and by Practical Action as the facilitator, Union-level officials stepped in to assist implementation using their formal and informal political ties and influence.

The UP also provided support in data gathering and for agricultural development, generally. In this last respect the Upazila officials have also proved supportive, meeting with Nadagari residents during the flood of 2004 and witnessing the level of community planning first-hand.

The various planning groups and participants in the villages proved catalytic in changing roles and creating links with other secondary stakeholders. Local government and service providers were crucial at all stage of pre-planning, planning and implementation and the Union- and Upazila-level Land Offices and Additional District Commissioner (ADC) at district level were very supportive in this respect. For instance, the Upazila Agricultural Coordination Committee (UACC) appears to be a very important interface between the various line departments and service providers and a potential audience for PAPD-type plans in future.

Practical Action found it possible to interact with and influence secondary stakeholders at these higher administrative levels and, in fact, the obscure land and water rights of the area necessitated this before meaningful planning and interventions could proceed. It was important that the communities recognized the potential of these stakeholders and were aware of the evolving relationships with them as their relevance increased and their function changed during the PAPD process.

Although there are undoubtedly political and administrative nodes that can permit or obstruct local-level planning such as PAPD, some of the opportunities and constraints encountered may have been a manifestation of the personal stance of individuals. In turn, this may relate to complex personal stakes relating to social and political capital and influence, or it may simply relate to enthusiasm for community-based rural development, distrust of NGOs, indifference etc. There are obvious consequences here for up-scaling forms of participatory action planning such as PAPD. While it is possible to make generalizations about the type of political, administrative or technical support required for community-based planning, it is impossible to guarantee its success. However, there are several themes that operate consistently in the charland setting and that require special attention by facilitators and those that will be implementing projects and programmes in the future. These nearly all relate to political and institutional isolation and the tendency for local, informal, political processes to fill a vacuum. These processes manifest themselves as local resource use conflict (irrespective of de jure statutory frameworks and policy regarding titlement etc.) and factionalism based on political and social influence. Such dynamics operate throughout rural Bangladesh but their isolated nature means that the modest demand-led change associated with the market and the private sector in other areas has not yet taken hold in the chars.

Farming futures

In the last few years there are signs that agricultural development policy is beginning to turn away from solely boosting production for global markets and there is now renewed interest in the viability of the small-scale farming sector. The cooperative or collective models of the past have been discarded and the model of the individual farmer as entrepreneur has come to the fore. Agricultural support services have been reformed as a consequence and are now being guided by more permissive 'multi-stakeholder' agriculture policies. Creative public–private agriculture extension models are proliferating.

With no new public resources available, however, the trend of stagnation and marginalization of agriculturally 'less favoured areas' with their difficult and resource-stressed farming conditions becomes ever more acute.[26] Poor people in such areas are particularly vulnerable to environmental shock and to the impact of conflict. Many remote rural areas which have long been neglected are now entering the public consciousness only because of accelerated rates of environmental degradation, famine or civil war (see Box 4.1).

Voices from the margins

The experiences of planning and consensus building with PAPD in the charlands should be relevant to other less favoured and remote rural areas across the

---

Box 4.1   Characteristics of remote rural areas

Bird *et al.* (2002) has defined four basic 'remote rural areas' according to their constraints:

- Areas with 'extreme' ecologies where infrastructure and communication is limited and difficult e.g. mountains, swamps, deserts, islands and charlands;
- Low-potential areas such as semi-arid areas, areas lacking topsoil, water resources and/ or are degraded (polluted, saline, with landmines etc.)
- Poverty pockets where social-political exclusion on the basis of language, identity (caste, religion, ethnicity etc.) or gender maintain significant proportions of the population in poverty
- Areas experiencing long-term conflict where violence and dislocation has undermined the resource base and the capacity of poor people to secure their livelihoods.

developing world. Donors are correctly turning to the issue of governance and how it may be possible to support civil society movements and institutional change that can benefit the poor longer term. A progression from micro-credit and technical options for agriculture towards an exploration of market linkages and engagement with government institutions and local influencers acknowledges this, and represents a rather more subtle use of agricultural technology. It transfers the emphasis from short-term support to production, to the longer-term development of democratic processes that can represent the poor and articulate their interests. A renewed vision of the collective opportunities associated with agricultural technologies can effectively catalyse new relations with weak but benign government service providers.

Supporting local production can open up new opportunities for NGOs and micro-level private sector initiatives in the whole chain of transportation and marketing. NGOs can broker relations with government and private sector service providers once improvements are sufficient to overcome transportation costs and the other constraints of isolation. Spontaneous developments, such as linkages between maize farmers and large-scale poultry producers, can embed themselves in the local economy.

The issue of who might resource and facilitate such changes remains unclear, however. In Bangladesh, the charland agricultural economy cannot be developed without support, without new assets or without facilitation. In Jamalpur, for example, the training and inputs for maize production were provided free in conjunction with a national agricultural research station based in the district. To bring about the livelihoods support to release energies for planning on a meaningful scale would require dedicated support to local/district NGOs within a broader programme of rural development. The experience of Practical Action in Bangladesh suggests that government technical and administrative institutions will come on board once early headway is made on agricultural initiatives with the resultant dynamism and demand from local groups.

Understanding the institutional environment for participatory planning

Prescriptive approaches to rural development have often yielded disappointing outcomes. It is important that a more reflective process is taken forward and one that can identify and work with supportive champions of change, whether these are the poor themselves or political stakeholders, entrepreneurs and other less vulnerable interests. As Rahman and Islam (2002) state:

> What of the vehicle(s) by which the goal of 'regenerating the local economy' is to be achieved? This is where a focus on local governance becomes of critical relevance. The cast of actors who matter here extend well beyond the traditional focus on local governments as they also cut across traditional sectoral or rural–urban boundaries. The challenge really is of multiple livelihoods, of linkages and a critical expansion of local opportunity frontiers, and of bringing within mainstream attention any categories of 'missing poor'. Such a menu of tasks does not fit easily within traditional sectoral

or decentralization approaches. What is required rather is a governance focus with a twist, namely, a primary orientation to livelihood issues and embracing the possibility of enlisting categories of actors beyond local governments per se.

Many development theorists and agencies are now acknowledging that the constraints to pro-poor change and representation are rooted in the institutional environment. In remote and neglected areas, where useful enabling institutions are often absent, development should be about challenging the political and social processes that have filled this vacuum but that often worked to constrain enterprise and prevent collaboration.

Recent research in Bangladesh and elsewhere has highlighted the role that pre-existing, but almost always overlooked, informal institutions play in legitimizing or obstructing change. These institutions may take the form of local platforms like mosque committees that will influence the management of village affairs. Other crucial informal institutions relate to established gender and livelihood roles or differences in status between different clans or *gusthi*. What is certain is that these institutions play a crucial part in the livelihoods of the poor, especially in areas where formal forms of support or representation are as poorly developed as they are in the Bangladesh charlands.

Encouragingly, when and where concerted efforts to decentralize occur, these institutions are likely to be joined by new players that contest existing mechanisms of management and access to benefits. Baumann and Farrington (2003) have described how decentralization policy in India has opened up new political space for civil society groups to challenge traditional authority and to meet the demands of local people: '...new leaders have become more aggressive in seeking schemes to benefit their (potential) supporters rather than accepting the usual 'solutions' from established power brokers.' As in Bangladesh, the district level is crucial in India because it is here that local demand eventually articulates with government funding and support. It is essential to recognize and promote this process and participatory planning must support the role of intermediaries as PAPD has done in the charlands.

A range of methods such as institutional mapping (see Bode, 2002), institutional process monitoring (Lewins, 2004) and tools to track most significant change (Davies, 2002) have been developed to help facilitators better understand the degree of 'fit' between agency objectives and the objectives of local people and the institutions that shape their livelihoods. Better institutional awareness allows facilitators to react to opportunities or problems as they arise and to acknowledge or confront 'difficult' issues publicly. In the context of PAPD and other forms of participatory action planning, a good understanding of local social and political processes allows for modification and experimentation.

Char-modified PAPD extended the planning period to accommodate confidence-building activities such as PTD and information gathering. This was a direct result of facilitator and community adaptation in the face of local realities.

Current and potential uses of PAPD

The PAPD model has been applied within numerous NRM projects in Bangladesh – mainly in the floodplain setting but also in the forestry setting, the coast and in the Chittagong Hill Tracts. To date, in excess of 20 NGOs have used the approach and government agencies such as the Department of Relief and Rehabilitation (DRR), the Water Resources Planning Organization (WARPO), the Department of Environment (DoE) and the Department of Fisheries (DoF) have utilized the principles or modified the approach. Internationally, projects in Cambodia, Vietnam and India have used PAPD in the inland and coastal fisheries sectors, principally as a tool for conflict resolution.

Interesting modifications are occurring on the fringes of the natural resource sector where the DRR have applied PAPD to the process of Community Risk Assessment (CRA) within the national Comprehensive Disaster Management Programme (CDMP). The intention here is to gauge local resilience to flooding and to develop contingency plans and institutions with local stakeholders.

CNRS has been central to this uptake and has developed a four-page policy brief and guide to disseminate the approach: 'PAPD – a tool for building consensus amongst stakeholders: a facilitator's guide'.

Practical Action will continue to apply and promote PAPD in the charlands. The principal vehicle will be the EC-funded Food Security – Bangladesh project (FOSHOL) to run with Action Aid and CARE from 2006–2010 and the 'Disappearing Lands' Project, working with communities displaced by river erosion in Gaibanda. Practical Action's 'Charlands Technical and Planning Manual' introduces PAPD and PTD options to technical GOs and NGOs working in the charlands.

There are several settings where PAPD and similar forms of participatory consensus building might contribute further:

- At the complex interface between fisheries and agriculture in the South Asian floodplain. PAPD has already been useful in overcoming existing conflict and establishing community-level institutions such as resource user groups. The facilitator plays a crucial role here, suggesting alternative management options that can link the interests of both fishing and farming interests, and explaining the cross-cutting benefits of community water management.
- As highlighted, Practical Action has extended the approach to the Bangladesh charlands where communities and secondary stakeholders rarely interact and where social conflict is common. The 'Bangladesh Poverty Reduction Strategy Paper' will encourage further regional rural development programmes that target marginalized areas such as the chars.
- Settings such as the peri-urban interface, where multiple stakeholders are required to identify mutually beneficial management interventions. These settings are more complex because the planning process must include a vertical chain of political stakeholders with varied objectives and a range of influence and power (see Bunting (2006) for a discussion of participatory action planning in the East Kolkata Wetlands).

- Conflict and consensus in water management is becoming ever more critical and watersheds represent another set of systems where the positions of multiple stakeholders are entrenched and where negotiation and mutual learning are required. The geographic scale and complexity involved requires vertical interaction between different administrative strata and perhaps between new platforms that represent users and other interests. Group-wise planning in isolation and in plenary will have a role here and facilitators can proactively engage civil society interests and supportive political stakeholders as potential 'drivers of change' (see Bdliya et al. (2006) for a discussion of participatory water resource planning in the Komadugu-Yobe Basin, Nigeria).

Quality participatory processes require political commitment and financial support. Many agencies in Bangladesh are openly acknowledging the poor performance of past projects and initiatives that have claimed a strong 'participatory' component. These same agencies seem keen to improve their performance in this regard but meaningful coverage might require adoption at the programme level.

Large NRM and rural development programmes would provide new users of participatory planning approaches like PAPD the time and flexibility required to make greatest impact and would enhance prospects of reaching large numbers of potential beneficiaries for several reasons: (1) it would provide an efficient structure for vetting and reaching new facilitators and providing ongoing support and advice; (2) it would utilize technical programme activities as an entry point to develop consensus and to build new institutional relations at local level or regional level; and (3) it would provide financial support for local plans and fund the cost of facilitation.

Finally, PAPD provides a framework that can help facilitators and participants to step outside the normal agency-to-community dynamic that characterizes different sectors and that results in narrow sets of agency prescribed outcomes and interventions. The process requires investing more in people and the process, trusting both staff and communities to find their way and to develop skills and confidence that can produce tangible and sustained pro-poor change.

Notes

1. These are exactly the characteristics that make ADR interesting in the context of consensus building and NRM in the developing world – see later.
2. Future Search has its roots in the Search Conference (Emery and Trist, 1973), large-scale community futures conferences (Schindler-Rainman and Lippitt, 1980), Open Space Technology (Owen, 1991), and Participative Strategic Planning Conferences (Jacobs, 1994).
3. In this respect, participatory rural appraisal (PRA) and planning could be interpreted as DIPs but as processes with a distinct function on behalf of development stakeholders rather than citizens, themselves.
4. The theoretical basis of AKIS is the social actor approach which sees people as central to an understanding of complex social constructs such as NRM systems (Röling 1996, Long and Van der Ploeg 1994, Long and Long 1992).
5. Platforms for resource-use negotiation are defined by Röling (1994) as statutory or voluntary decision-making bodies dealing with specific sets of NRM problems and representing interdependent stakeholders.
6. The manual is based on guidelines developed by the Overseas Development Institute for the management of community-based natural resource projects in Fiji and Papua New Guinea, funded by the DFID and organized by the United Kingdom Foundation for the Peoples of the South Pacific.
7. Moore and Santosa (1995) describe the limited success of the Indonesian government in its recent attempts to promote the traditional dispute resolution practice of *musyawarah* for use within a national framework. After independence, the government of Indonesia attempted to shift dispute resolution away from village-based practices to formal judicial and bureaucratic institutions. However, because the traditional systems had been so effectively eroded within local government, bureaucrats did not recognize or understand the principles of *musyawarah* and its role in reaching consensus (*muafakat*) when they were reintroduced.
8. Uphoff was attempting an explanation of the scale of consensus and the surprising speed and success of an irrigation project at Gal Oya, Sri Lanka.
9. In 1978 the USA adopted a traditional practice of Egyptian village conflict resolution (the *Mulakah*) to broker agreement between President Sadat of Egypt and President Begin of Israel (Miall et al., 1999).
10. Hall (1976), for example, distinguishes between the two extremes of an American 'low context' perspective to negotiation and a Japanese 'high context' perspective. Typical characteristics of negotiation in low-context cultures are an emphasis on the self, autonomy, direct (face-to-face) engagement and competitive strategies. Conversely, high-context cultures emphasize collective identity, inclusion, indirect engagement and collaborative strategies. Generally, it is the developed and multi-institutional cultures that are low context, although Hall considers the Japanese

perspective a high context one: 'Low context cultures generally refer to groups characterised by individualism, overt communication and heterogeneity. The United States, Canada and central and northern Europe are described as areas where low context cultural practices are most in evidence. High context cultures feature collective identity-focus, covert communication and homogeneity. This approach prevails in Asian countries including Japan, China and Korea as well as Latin American countries.'

11. Assets and livelihoods options are virtually synonymous with Sens's (1981) *endowments* and *entitlements*.

12. In this regard, Baumann (2000) argues that 'political capital' should form a sixth livelihoods asset rather than represented as an external entity within the surrounding environment of PIPs.

13. Initially 'Investigation of livelihood strategies and resource use patterns in floodplain production systems based on rice and fish in Bangladesh' (Project R6756) and later 'Methods for consensus building for management of common property resources' (Project R7562) – both supported by the Natural Resources Systems Programme of the UK Department for International Development. CNRS is a research-centred NGO with broad experience of NRM projects and advocacy in Bangladesh.

14. CNRS has developed PAPD training material that outlines the workshop activities in greater detail (see http://www.cnrs-bd.org).

15. Another example is the King Mahendra Nature Conservation Trust which has promoted a collaborative and integrated approach to the management of the Ampuna Conservation Area in Nepal (see Borrini-Feyerabend et al., 2000). Decision-making committees operate at local, regional and national levels to develop suitable agreements and management tasks under the facilitation of *lami* (matchmakers). Stakeholders have direct input but their participation is fixed in the context of national or international conservation commitments and objectives.

16. In Bangladesh, fishing and farming interests have too often been viewed as mutually exclusive, by NGOs and government agencies alike. Although water use conflict is common, PAPD helps facilitators and participants develop interventions that can provide benefits that cross-cut interest groups.

17. The overlap of the formal and informal institutional network should be stressed. As Bode (2002) states: 'Formal institutions, the vehicles through which the devolution of allocation over resources and benefits are to be achieved, however, operate within the context of local political culture and the firmly entrenched social practices …the *salish*, for instance.'

18. Literally 'village government' the Gram Sharkar system was introduced in 1982. Based on the Indian Panchayat system, the intention was to devolve decision-making power to a council of 12–13 elected representatives at village level. One member of the council is then elected to represent the village at Upazilla level. In both villages, the councils were heavily politicized, deemed ineffectual and generally held in low esteem.

19. Such 'uxorilocal' marriages contrast with a more 'virilocal' tradition; in which women move in with the male family and become part of their *gusthi*.

20. The residency of participants also mattered greatly. Practical Action's suggestion to include extension officers in the PAPD committee was challenged by local participants on the grounds that these individuals were not local residents.

21. In both Nandina and Nadagari, Practical Action has developed the technical skills, knowledge and linkages of several local volunteers (rural community extensionists) for fisheries, livestock and agriculture-related support.

22. The water body management committee (WBMC) at Nandina developed basic membership and denoted roles but the process was allowed to evolve with little interference from the Practical Action team. Careful facilitation enabled the community to modify the committee and make it more representative of the poorest.

23. Secondary stakeholders such as Union Parishad representatives and livestock extensionists were more motivated to participate after initial local planning had resulted in provisional plans.

24. In this case, the Assistant District Commissioner was found to be responsive to and supportive of community planning within the project and his support opened up opportunities to influence the Land Registry agencies further up the bureaucratic the chain.

25. Social capital, and hence the potential of consensual planning, tend to be weak in displaced 'communities'. The level of social capital is particularly low in transitory settlements or refugee camps where pre-existing social bonds are lacking or have been broken, for instance.

26. 'Less favoured areas' are defined as those where a relatively low level of income is realized due to difficult physical conditions and/or lack of infrastructure and service support and where private decision makers would not start to invest under present and expected future conditions (Oskam et al., 2004).

References

Agrawal, A. and Gibson, C.C. (1999) Enchantment and Disenchantment: The Role of Community in Natural Resource Conservation. *World Development*, **27** (4), pp. 629–649.

Barr, J.J.F., Dixon, P.-J., Rahman M.M., Islam, A., Zuberi, M.I., McGlynn, A.A., and Ghosh, G.P. (2000) *Report on a participatory systems-based process for identification of improved natural resource management for better floodplain livelihoods*. London: DFID, NRSP.

Barr, J.J.F. and Dixon, P.-J. (2001) Methods for consensus building for management of common property resources. Final Technical Report R7562. University of Newcastle, UK: Centre for Land Use and War Resources Research.

Baumann, P. (2000) Sustainable livelihoods and social capital: arguments and evidence from decentralization and natural resource management in India. Working Paper 136. Overseas Development Institute, London.

Baumann, P. and Farrington J. (2003) Decentralising natural resource management: lessons from local government reform in India. Natural Resource Perspectives, **86**, June.

Bdliya, H.H., Barr, J.J.F and Fraser, S. (2006) *1. Institutional failures in the management of critical water resources: the case of the Komadugu-Yobe Basin in Nigeria* or, *2. Persistence and opportunism – the realities of trying to improve water governance in West Africa*. Paper for the seminar Water Governance – New Perspectives and Directions, 20–21st February, Bradford, UK.

Bertocci, P.J. (1996) Models of solidarity, structures of power: the politics of community in rural Bangladesh, in *Ideology and Interest: The dialectics of politics. Political Anthropology Yearbook,* ed. Aronoff, M.J., pp. 97–125, Transaction Books, reprinted in Bertocci, P.J., *The Politics of community and culture in Bangladesh: Selected essays*. CSS: Dhaka University.

Bird, K., Hulme, D., Moore, K. and Shepherd, A. (2002) Chronic Poverty and Remote Rural Areas, CPRC Working Paper No 13.

Bode, B. (2002) *In Pursuit of Power: Local Elites and Union-Level Governance in Rural Northwestern Bangladesh*, Care Bangladesh.

Borrini-Feyerabend, G. (1997) *Beyond fences: seeking social sustainability in conservation.* Gland, Switzerland: IUCN.

Borrini-Feyerabend, G., Farvar, T.M., Nguinguiri, J.C. and Ndangang, V.A. (2000) *Co-management of natural resources: Organising, negotiating and learning-by-doing*. Heidelberg, Germany: Kasperag Verlag.

Bunting, S. (2006) Evaluating action planning for enhanced natural resource management in peri-urban Kolkata. Final Technical Report R8365: University of Stirling, UK: Institute of Aquaculture.

Burgess, G. and Burgess, H. (1996) Consensus Building for Environmental Advocates. [Online] http://www.colorado.edu/conflict/hwltap9.htm.

CARE (2002) *The North West institutional analysis: summary*. CARE Go-Interfish Project. CARE Bangladesh.

Carney, D. (1999) *Sustainable Rural Livelihoods: what contribution can we make?* Papers presented at the Department for International Development's Natural Resources Advisers' Conference, July 1998. DFID, UK.

Castro, A.P. (1996) *Indigenous knowledge and conflict management: exploring local perspectives and mechanisms for dealing with community forestry disputes.* Paper prepared for the FAO, Community Forestry Unit, for the Global Electronic Conference on Addressing Natural Resource Conflicts through Community Forestry, January–April.

Center for Democracy and Governance – USAID (2000) *Alternative Dispute Resolution Practitioner's Guide. Technical Publications Series.* **15.**

Cohn, B. (1967) Some notes on law and change in North India, in *Law and Warfare*, ed. Bohannan, P., pp 139–159. Garden City, NY: The Natural History Press.

Danzig, R. (1973) Toward the creation of a complementary, decentralized system of criminal justice. *Stanford Law Review* **26**, pp. 1–54.

Davies, R. (2002) *Improved Representations of Change Processes: Improved Theories of Change.* Paper presented at Seville 2002: 5th Biennial Conference of the European Evaluation Society. Three Movements in Contemporary Evaluation: Learning, Theory and Evidence, October.

DFID (2000) *Sustainable Livelihoods Guidance Sheets.* UK: Department for International Development.

Emery, F.E. and Trist, E.L. (1973) *Towards a Social Ecology.* New York: Plenum.

Engel, P.G.H. and Salomon, M.L. (1997) *Facilitating Innovation for Development. A RAAKS Resource Box.* Amsterdam: Royal Tropical Institute.

Fisher, R. and Ury, W. (1981) *Getting to Yes.* Boston: Houghton Mifflin Company.

Gibbs, J. (1963) The Kpelle moot: a therapeutic model for the informal settlement of disputes. *Africa,* **33**, pp. 1–11.

Gujja, B., Pimbert, M.P. and Shah, M., (1998) Village voices challenging wetland-management policies: PRA experiences from Pakistan and India, in *Whose voice? Participatory research and policy change*, ed. Holland, J. and Blackburn, J. London: IT Publications.

Hall, E.T. (1976) *Beyond Culture.* Garden City, NY: Anchor.

Habermas, J. (1984) Reason and the Rationalization of Society, Volume 1 of *The Theory of Communicative Action*, English translation by Thomas McCarthy. Boston: Beacon Press.

Holmes, T. and Scoones, I. (2000) Participatory Policy Processes: experiences from North and South. IDS Working Paper 113. Brighton: Institute of Development Studies, University of Sussex.

Innes, J.E (2000) Evaluating Consensus Building, in *The Consensus Building Handbook – A Comprehensive Guide to Reaching Agreement,* ed. Susskind, L., McKearnon, S. and Thomas-Larmer, J., pp. 631–675, Thousand Oaks, CA: Sage Publications.

Islam, S.A. (2002) The informal institutional framework in rural Bangladesh, in *Hands not land: how livelihoods are changing rural Bangladesh,* pp. 97–104. Dhaka: Bangladesh Institute of Development Studies.

Jacobs. R.J. (1994) *Real Time Strategic Change.* San Francisco: Berrett-Koehler Publishers.

Kaner, S. (1996) *Facilitator's Guide to Participatory Decision Making.* San Francisco: New Society Publishers, British Columbia with Community at Work.

Keohane, R.O. and Ostrom, E. (1995) *Local Commons and Global Interdependence: Heterogeneity and Co-operation in Two Domains.* London: Sage Publications.

Kramer, R. M. and Messick, D. M. (1995) *Negotiation as a Social Process.* Thousand Oaks, CA: Sage Publications.

Krishna, A. and Shrader, E. (1999) *Social Capital Assessment Tool (SCAT)*. Paper for the Conference on Social Capital and Poverty Reduction. 22–24 June. Washington: World Bank.

Leach, M, Mearns, R, and Scoones, I. (1997) Environmental Entitlements: A Framework for Understanding the Institutional Dynamics of Environmental Change. IDS Discussion Paper 359. Brighton: University of Sussex.

Lewins, R. (2004) Integrated floodplain management – institutional environments and participatory methods. DFID NRSP Project R8195, Final Technical Report.

Long, N. and Long, A., eds. (1992) *Battlefields of Knowledge: the interlocking of theory and practice in research and development*. London: Routledge.

Long, N., and van der Ploeg, J.D. (1994) Heterogeneity, actor and structure: towards a reconstitution of the concept of structure, in *Rethinking social development: theory, research and practice*, ed. Booth, D., pp. 62–89, London: Longman.

Lund, B., Morris, C. and LeBaron Duryea, M. (1994) *Conflict and Culture: Report of the Multiculturalism and Dispute Resolution Project*. Victoria, BC: University of Victoria Institute of Dispute Resolution.

MacNaughton, A.L. and Brune, G.J. (1997) *Mediating sustainable development conflicts in warm and humid petrochemical zones*. Paper presented at the ABA/IBA Conference on Development, the Environment and Dispute Resolution in the Americas: New Directions for the Private Sector.

Miall, H., Ramsbotham, O. and Woodhouse, T. (1999) *Contemporary Conflict Resolution*. Oxford/Cambridge, Polity Press.

Moore, C.J. (1996) *The Mediation Process: Practical Strategies for Resolving Conflict*. Chichester: Jossey-Bass.

Moore, C. and Priscoli, J.D. (1989) *Executive summary on ADR procedures*. Fort Belvoir, VA: Institute for water Resources, US Army Corps of Engineers.

Moore, C. and Santosa, M. (1995) Developing appropriate environmental conflict management procedures in Indonesia: integrating traditional and modern approaches. *Cultural Survival Quarterly* **19**, pp. 23–29.

Nader, L. (1995) Civilization and its negotiations, in *Understanding Disputes*, ed. Caplan, P., pp. 65–82. Oxford: Berg.

Nader, L. and Todd, H. (1978) *The Disputing Process*. Berkley: University of California Press.

Oskam, A.J., Komen, M.H.C., Wobst, P. and Yalew, A. (2004) Trade policies and development of less-favoured areas: evidence from the literature. *Food Policy* **29** (4), pp. 445–466.

Owen, H. (1991) *Riding the Tiger: Doing Business in a Transforming World*. Potomoc, MD: Abbott Publishing.

Pelletier, D., Kraak, V., McCullum, C., Uusitalo, U., and Rich, R. (1999) The shaping of collective values through deliberative democracy: an empirical study from New York's North Country. *Policy Sciences* **32**, pp. 103–131.

Pimbert, M.P. and Pretty, J.N. (1994) *Participation, People and the Management of National Parks and Protected Areas: Past Failures and Future Promise*. Geneva: United Nations Research Institute for Social Development.

Priscoli, J.D. (1990) Public Involvement, Conflict Management and Dispute Resolution in Water Resources and Environmental Decision-Making. IWR Working Paper 90-ADR-WP-2. Fort Belvoir, VA: Institute for Water Resources, US Army Corps of Engineers.

Pruitt, O. and Carnevale, P. (1993) *Negotiation in social conflict*. Buckingham, UK: Open University Press.

Pruitt, D. and Rubin, J. (1986) *Social Conflict: Escalation, Stalemate and Settlement*. New York: Random House.

Rabbie, M. (1994) *Conflict Resolution and Ethnicity*. Westport, CT: Greenwood Press.

Rahman, H.Z. and Islam, R.A. (2002) *Local Governance and Community Capacities, the Search for New Frontiers*. India: Dhaka UP.

Rijsberman, F. (1999) *Conflict management and consensus building for integrated coastal management in Latin America and the Caribbean*. Technical Paper Series. Inter-American Development Bank, Sustainable Development Department. December, pp. 1–51.

Röling, N.G. (1992) The Emergence of Knowledge Systems Thinking, in *Knowledge and Policy: The International Journal of Knowledge Transfer and Utilization*, 5 (1), pp. 42–64.

Röling, N.G. (1994) Platforms for decision-making about ecosystems, in *The Future of the land: mobilising and integrating knowledge for land use options*, eds. Fresco, L.O., Stroosnijder, L., Bouma, J. and van Keulen, H., pp. 385–393. Chichester: Wiley.

Röling, N. (1996) Creating human platforms to manage natural resources: first results of a research programme. *Agricultural RandD at the Crossroads – merging systems research and social actor approaches,* ed. Budelman, A. pp. 149–156. Amsterdam: KIT Publishers.

Schindler-Rainman, E. and Lippitt, R. (1980) *Building the Collaborative Community: Mobilizing Citizens for Action*. Irvine: University of California.

Scialabba, N. (ed.) (1998) *Integrated Coastal Area Management and Agriculture, Forests and Fisheries. FAO Guidelines*. Rome: Environment and Natural Resource Service, FAO.

Sen, A. (1981) *Poverty and Famines: an Essay on Entitlement and Deprivation*. Oxford: Oxford University Press.

Steins, N.A. and Edwards, V.M. (1998) Platforms for collective action in multiple-use CPRs. Discussion paper for the 7th IASCP Conference, Vancouver.

Thompson, L., Peterson, E., and Kray, L. (1995) Social context in negotiation: an information processing perspective, in *Negotiation as a Social Process*, ed. Kramer, R.M and Messick, D.M., pp. 5–36. Thousand Oaks, CA: Sage.

Thornton, P. (2002) The formal institutional framework of rural livelihoods on Bangladesh, in *Hands not Land: How Livelihoods are Changing in Rural Bangladesh*, ed. Toufique K and Turton, C. Dhaka: DFID/BIDS.

Uphoff, N. (1996) Understanding the world as a heterogeneous whole: insights into systems from work on irrigation. *Systems Research* 13 (1), pp. 3–12.

Walker, P. (1999) *How to Design a Community Vision*. Central Briefing Document. Centre for Participation, London: New Economics Foundation.

Warner, M. (1997) 'Consensus' participation: an example for protected areas planning. *Public Administration and Development* 17, pp. 413–432.

Warner, M. (1999) *Managing conflict and building consensus in rural livelihood projects: strategies, principles, tools and training material*. London: Overseas Development Institute.

Weisbord, M.R. and Janoff, S. (1995) *Future Search. An Action Guide to Finding Common Ground in Organisations and Communities*. San Francisco: Berrett-Koehler Publishers.

Westergaard, K. and Hossain, A. (1997) Mobilisation for khas land, two experiences from Pabna, in Bangladesh in the 1990s, Selected Studies, ed. Schendel, W.V. and Westergaard, K., pp. 81–99, University Press, Dhaka.

Westergaard, K. and Hossein, A. (2002) Local Institutions in Bangladesh, An Analysis of Civil Society and Local Elections, in *Contesting Political Space for Poverty Reduction*, ed. Webster, N. and Engberg Petersen, L. London: Zed Books.

Wood, G. (2003) Staying secure, staying poor: The 'Faustian Bargain'. *World Development*, 31 (3) pp. 455–471.

Index